MY JOURNEY WITH

*Farrah*

# MY JOURNEY WITH

### A Story of Life,
### Love, and Friendship

Alana Stewart

wm

WILLIAM MORROW

*An Imprint of* HarperCollins*Publishers*

MY JOURNEY WITH FARRAH. Copyright © 2009 by Alana Stewart. All rights reserved.
Printed in the United States of America. No part of this book may be used or reproduced
in any manner whatsoever without written permission except in the case of brief quotations
embodied in critical articles and reviews. For information address HarperCollins
Publishers, 10 East 53rd Street, New York, NY 10022.

HarperCollins books may be purchased for educational, business, or sales promotional use.
For information please write: Special Markets Department, HarperCollins Publishers,
10 East 53rd Street, New York, NY 10022.

FIRST EDITION

Library of Congress Cataloging-in-Publication Data has been applied for.

ISBN 978-0-06-196058-1

09  10  11  12  13      WBC/RRD      10  9  8  7  6  5  4  3  2  1

To my beautiful friend and soul-sister Farrah, who has so deeply affected my life and will live in my heart forever.

And to my children, Ashley, Kimberly, and Sean, who live in my heart always.

A friend is more than an ally. As it says in the I Ching, even thieves have alliances. Alliances come and go.

A friend, however, is more than that. In a world where love has become so cheap, friendship is a love that refuses to be cheapened. It means more than just lending a hand, or sharing the easier niceties of an easy existence. A friendship that is always easy is a friendship that is not yet beautified.

A friend is willing to take a stand for you . . . even when sitting something out would be easier. A friend has your back . . . refusing to ignore it when someone else is subtly stabbing it. A friend can stay up all night and celebrate your victories, but remains awake with you unflinchingly in the hour of your agony.

A real friend will rework their schedule, fly an extra mile, spend capital, proactively support your dreams and take seriously your visions. An easy friend is often a false friend, but a *real* friend . . . a true, fiercely loyal friend . . . if ever there was a pure and precious diamond of the heart, that is it.

—MARIANNE WILLIAMSON

# CONTENTS

# A NOTE FROM THE AUTHOR

———◦———

W HEN FARRAH AND I WERE ON ONE OF OUR EARLY TRIPS TO
Germany getting her cancer treatment, I went to this little
gift shop, the Summer Haus. I bought a book, written in German,
about two friends, and I gave it to her back at the clinic. We flipped
through it. Neither of us could understand a word of German, but
we got the gist of it: it was about two women and their journey of
friendship. Farrah turned to me and said, "You know, you should
do a book like this . . . about us." I didn't think much more about it
at the time. But I never forgot it.

When the opportunity to do this book was actually presented
to me, I had to think long and hard about it. In fact, I agonized over
the decision. During the past two or more years that Farrah and I
had been on this journey together, I'd protected her like a mother
lioness guards her cub. Now was I doing the right thing by sharing many of our private moments? Even though Farrah had originally encouraged me to write this book? Her health took a turn for
the worse, and I could no longer seek her input.

So I turned to Ryan for his advice. He was positive and supportive. "You have to do it," he said emphatically. "There will be
lots of people writing books about her. Yours will be the truth,

and it will be a wonderful tribute to her. You *have* to do it!" He was extremely reassuring.

Now I feel comfortable with my decision; that it will honor Farrah in the way that Ryan and I both envisioned. I know this book would have made her proud. My dream was that, by the time this book was out, she'd be better and I could present her with the first copy of it. Sadly, that won't happen now.

I prayed and meditated and asked God to show me the highest sense of right. What I got was that this was my gift to others, to share through my eyes the incredible courage and spirit of Farrah. I hoped I could, perhaps, give some support and encouragement not only to people fighting a disease, but also to those loved ones and friends walking the path with them. I had never experienced anything like this before, and there were many times I felt inadequate and frightened. I'm sure this must be a common feeling.

These entries are a tribute to the value of friendship; whether it's helping a friend who's fighting cancer or any other challenge. By putting myself aside temporarily and being there for someone I loved, I learned a wealth of spiritual and life lessons that changed me forever. One of the most important, and perhaps the most powerful, spiritual teachings in the world is selflessness; something that wasn't at the top of my "To Do" list. Doing something kind for another person can transform you in unimaginable ways. I will always be grateful to my beautiful friend Farrah for allowing me to travel this journey with her. What started out as my gift to her became her gift to me.

A portion of the proceeds from this book will be donated to The Farrah Fawcett Foundation to support cancer research.

If you wish to make a donation to The Farrah Fawcett Foundation, you may do so at the following address:

**P.O. Box 6478**
**Beverly Hills, CA 90212**

The bond between women friends is all-powerful and not to be taken lightly. But the bond between Alana and Farrah is like nothing I've ever seen between two women. They grew together like vines.

—RYAN O'NEAL

I was always the small brunette in the middle— bookended by two very headstrong Texas beauties, equally loyal and dependable—the stuff that bonds us through good and bad times. It would take these qualities to sustain Farrah and Alana on their journey through what I call the *cancer abyss*. Farrah's courage was matched only by Alana's commitment to stay at Farrah's side, to comfort and encourage her during her struggle to beat this damn disease. We, Farrah's friends, cannot thank Alana enough for all her sacrifice—time away from her home, her children, and her doggies. *My Journey with Farrah* fills and enriches our spirits as Farrah soars with the angels.

—TINA SINATRA

M EN COME AND GO—GOD KNOWS THEY CERTAINLY have in my life—but girlfriends are forever. I have a lot of girlfriends, but only a few very, very close ones. And in the middle of that select circle, I considered Farrah Fawcett to be my soul-sister. We would have done anything for each other. But I never anticipated that our lives would become intertwined in the way that they did. I never imagined I would walk this path with her.

The first time I laid eyes on Farrah was in the 1970s. We hadn't formally met yet, but I spotted her on a commercial audition and thought she was absolutely beautiful (she later told me she thought the same about me). We both arrived in L.A. around the same time. She came straight from Corpus Christi, Texas, and I had been modeling in New York and Paris. We kept bumping into each other at these casting calls, and at first our friendship was casual: a smile, a nod, a quick "How's it going?"

A few years later, we were no longer just girls hustling for work in Hollywood. By then I was separated from my first husband, George Hamilton, and had been acting in a few TV series, while Farrah was a huge star, an icon, thanks to *Charlie's Angels*. I went to Palm Springs to play in a celebrity tennis tournament with my friend Valerie Perrine, and when we arrived, there were young kids lined up outside the tennis club, screaming Farrah's name. Truth be told, Valerie and I had no business being there. We couldn't even play tennis! We'd bought the shortest tennis shorts we could find, hoping they would distract people from how bad we were. Each of us had a pro partner, and I pity the poor guy who got me. When a ball came sailing at me, I dove for the ground, narrowly missing getting smacked in the head. Farrah, on the other hand, was a powerful and graceful tennis player, a natural athlete, and, of course, she won the tournament while barely breaking a sweat. How easy it would have been to hate someone so seemingly perfect, but all you could do was love her. She was so warm, so approachable, so down-to-earth. People were just naturally drawn to her like moths to a bright flame.

We met again and really bonded in 1979, when I was pregnant with my daughter, Kimberly, and married to my second husband, Rod Stewart. Rod and I were at Countess Marina Cicogna's house for a dinner, and she sat Farrah, Ryan, Rod, and me together. Farrah and I hit it off immediately, and quickly discovered that we had a lot in common, especially our Texas roots. We also discovered another interesting connection: we were both part American Indian. I'm a one-quarter Cherokee-Choctaw mix, and Farrah was part Choctaw. Farrah's mother always said the Choctaw were the lazy Indians! I've heard that if you're from the same tribe, you have a blood tie; maybe that's why we eventually became so spiritually connected.

Ultimately, what I loved about Farrah from day one was that

there was no BS. What you saw was what you got, and I found that refreshing—an actual down-home girl in Hollywood.

After that dinner, we started up a *real* friendship. She was working so much in those days that we couldn't spend a lot of time together, but when we did, we had a ball. Being around her felt like being home in Texas. We used to joke that all we needed were the big pink rollers in our hair. We'd go down to Ryan's beach house, get massages, manicures, and pedicures, and lie in the sun reading fashion magazines—just two friends forgetting about life for twenty-four hours. We hung out, we ate Tex-Mex, we baked homemade pies. Farrah was always such fun. She embraced life more than anyone I've ever known.

Over the years, there was rarely a birthday party or a New Year's that we didn't celebrate together. As time went on, Farrah and I became even closer, even as our lives took very different paths. I got married and was busy having babies (Kimberly, Sean, and Ashley), while she had the kind of thriving acting career I had always dreamed about. In 1984 when Rod and I broke up, Farrah and Ryan were there to comfort and support me. In 1986, before her son, Redmond, was born, I threw her baby shower. But through it all, she stayed the same Farrah. She raised her son without a nanny, helping him with his homework and cooking dinner almost every night. As we got older, and Redmond and my sons all struggled with drug and alcohol problems, she and I bonded even more in our pain and concern over our boys. In the beginning of our relationship, Farrah was private and guarded with her emotions; eventually we could talk about anything.

Farrah was the last person I ever thought would get cancer. It never remotely crossed my mind that such a thing would happen. She was always too strong, too healthy, too full of life. I always thought she was one of the most fortunate women I knew.

She had it all—or so it seemed. Life is fragile; it changes in a heartbeat. One day Farrah was fine, the next she was not. Yet through it all, I never heard her question "Why me?" I never saw her act like a victim. She made the decision to fight her cancer and never wavered. It was very hard—sometimes unbearable—to watch my friend suffer, but I was in awe of her ferocious determination. Sometimes I thought it was her stubbornness and sheer willpower that got her through it. Other times I marveled at her heroism in waging war with an enemy who gave no hint as to where it might attack next—or how much it would destroy in its path. We went to Germany together to try to find a cure, a miracle, some hope in the face of hopelessness. And it was there that my friend handed me her camera and asked me to video what she was going through. I had no idea how to use a camera, and she showed me how to press the little RECORD button. So it began.

Over the next two years, there were more trips to Germany for treatments. My life took a backseat to Farrah's battle with cancer. I would drop everything, leave my family and my dogs and my home, and hop a plane at a moment's notice if she needed me. I felt like she was also my family, that it was something I had to do and wanted to do, and that I would worry about myself later. We tried, us tough Texas girls, to keep it together, to laugh and retain our sense of humor.

In the beginning, we truly thought there would be a happy

ending; she'd find a cure, she'd be healthy again. It seemed not just plausible but probable. But life took an unforeseen turn. As her disease progressed, Farrah could have given up. Truthfully, I might have if I were in her shoes. Instead, she found a greater purpose. The video that I started filming that day in Germany turned into something bigger—a documentary that would shed light on cancer and encourage others who were suffering, as well as show the world that there were alternative forms of treatment. Farrah felt very committed to speaking up and saying that we needed more studies and more research. She wanted to bring awareness to her type of cancer, and she wanted to give people hope. Above all, she wanted to say, "Don't give up—no matter what anyone tells you—keep on fighting."

I also found a greater calling in this experience, and through it learned some invaluable life lessons. One of the most important is the basic foundation of all spiritual teachings: the power of giving. When you unselfishly do something for someone else, when you get beyond yourself, out of your head, and out of your own way, God solves your problems for you. Many people ask me how I could have put my life on hold for three years to be with Farrah all that time. I don't see it as a sacrifice. I see it as simply being there for my friend, and it's ended up being a blessing and a gift for me. Farrah had been an inspiration to so many people, not just those who have cancer but people in other challenging situations. The letters of gratitude poured in by the thousands every week. I feel privileged to have been part of all this. I am a different person, a better person, because of it. As sad and painful as the journey was, it gave me a new perspective on who I am and what is really important in life. And this perspective has turned my life around in ways I could never have envisioned.

I have kept journals since I was nine years old, and I would sometimes read Farrah what I had written in them. She loved my writing. "You're such a good writer," she'd say encouragingly. "You must keep doing this." I did. I would diligently pour out my feelings, fears, and frustrations in my journal, and I soon realized how much the most recent volumes, just like my life these past three years, were about Farrah and her courageous battle with cancer. Paging through the frantically scribbled entries—some written in the wee hours of the morning when I was too stressed to sleep—I found that book which Farrah had suggested about two friends and their journey together. I suspect Farrah knew it was in there all along.

What follows is my journal of these past three years—what I saw, what I felt, what I was going through with Farrah, and how it was affecting my own life. Sometimes I wrote every day. Other times life was too hectic and the weeks flew by without my writing. But put them all together, and what you have is a celebration of our friendship as much as it is a chronicle of cancer treatment. Our relationship grew and deepened because of this experience we went through together. It was the bright spot in the midst of all the darkness. I don't know what my life will be like without Farrah in it. I can't imagine it. I can't go there. But I do know I won't have anyone to make pecan pies with me on Christmas. What I do have, and what I want to share, is the memory of a friendship of thirty years— and this, the greatest and the last adventure that we went on together.

*A happier time.*

*This was Farrah's favorite picture of us. She kept it in a frame by her bedside, as I do. She liked the way we look in it . . . suntanned and rested. It was such a quiet, peaceful trip. We were able to get away from the world and lie in the sun. It was New Year's Eve and everyone else went out, but we stayed in and celebrated with each other . . . and the cook. I made this drink that turned out to be our favorite, a Yellowbird: it was coconut rum and pineapple juice. We had that in lieu of champagne. At midnight we toasted each other. Just looking at this photo evokes such happy memories: two best friends toasting each other, our friendship, and the promise of what a new year would bring. It's how I like to think of Farrah: happy, healthy, hopeful. It was before all of this happened to us, before her cancer, before our journey. If I close my eyes, I can see us back in the Bahamas, lying out in the warm sun, gazing at the clear turquoise waters, and walking barefoot along the pink sand beaches.*

*Whenever I was caught up in the stress and strain and agony of watching my friend go through this horrific battle, and I started to forget, all I needed to do was look at this photo . . . and I was back in the Bahamas with Farrah again.*

# HORRIBLE NEWS

I've been here in Germany now for two weeks, at the Leonardis Clinic, which is nestled in the foothills of the beautiful Bavarian Alps. I brought my son Sean here to get treated for his ADD and learning disabilities. We were soon joined by my ex-husband George Hamilton, my daughter Kimberly, and my friend Cher.

It's a great place. The first time I was here, George sent me for my birthday in 2005 as a present. He insisted that I go—I didn't want to—but he said, "No, you have to do this for yourself." I was suffering from chronic fatigue and the accompanying depression. The clinic helped me a great deal. Leonardis is well known for cutting-edge cancer treatments, but it also specializes in other health problems. A few of my friends had seen what good results I had after coming here, and they decided they would try it as well.

Kim came into my room this morning, visibly upset. "Mom, does Farrah have cancer?"

"What? Where did you hear that?"

"I read it on the Internet."

I was furious. "Of course not, that's ridiculous. It's just that bullshit stuff they always print about her." The tabloids have been writing garbage about Farrah for as long as I've known her, but this rumor was too upsetting. I called Farrah just to make sure. I waited a rather long time for her to come to the phone, and I suddenly had a sinking feeling in my gut.

When she picked up, I said, "Honey, it's Alana. Listen, Kimberly just told me she read something about you on the Internet. It's not true, is it?"

There was a long pause as I held my breath.

"It's true," she said softly. "It happened so quickly." Then she started to cry. She was trying to be brave, but with me, she could let it all out.

I was afraid to ask, but I had to: "Honey, what do the doctors say?"

Her voice took on a stronger, more optimistic tone. "The doctors tell me they have great success with this kind of tumor, but it's very aggressive, and they have to start chemo and radiation right away." No time to breathe or even to digest this horrible news; no time to waste. Is that how it works? One day you're fine, the next day you're fighting for your life? On top of it all, she told me she has a 50/50 chance of losing her hair. But I guess hair becomes secondary with what she's going through. Still, the hair, *her* hair.

"I'm supposed to stay another week, but I'll come back right away," I said. "I'll be there."

After I hung up, I lay awake for hours with thoughts swirling around in my mind. How did this happen? Why? She's been through so much—her son Redmond's struggles with drugs the last few years, her mom dying recently, Ryan's battle with leukemia. It doesn't seem fair. I've been worried about her for a long time. She's had so much stress in her life lately and she always takes care of everyone else at the expense of herself. She spent months in Texas at her mother's bedside, neglecting her own health. Time and time again I've seen her ignore her own symptoms when someone she loves needs her.

I don't want to watch my best friend go through this. I want to cry but I can't seem to. I feel numb and scared. But this isn't about me. I have to do whatever I can to help her.

### October 10, 2006

It's 6:30 A.M. and I got home from Germany the day before yesterday. I can't sleep; I keep thinking about Farrah. Tina [Sinatra] and I spoke to her on a three-way call yesterday for a long time. She has started her chemo and radiation. She sounded a little weak, but calm and strong and accepting of what she has to go through.

"The doctors told me it's not going to be easy," Farrah said. "They told me, 'You're going to come to a time halfway through this treatment when you want to quit. But you have to keep going.' " I know Farrah and her will and determination. She won't quit, no matter what. She wants to beat this.

Tina and I are going to see her tomorrow and I asked her what I could bring. "Your minestrone soup," she said. So when we hung up, I drove to Whole Foods to get the vegetables for her favorite soup.

I used to have this belief that people who were famous or bigger than life were immune from these kind of things, but I've watched too many people who I thought were invincible, who seemingly had it all, experience life's hardships and tragedies just like everyone else. No one is immune from life, not even an icon like Farrah, the golden girl of the seventies. Any one of us can get a phone call that changes our life in a flash. So many things can happen, to anyone, any time. Just writing about it I feel frozen with fear. I want some guarantee from God, from the universe, that Farrah will be okay, that I'll be safe, that the people I love will be safe. But there are no guarantees.

My friend Lesley says we have to stay in the present, live every moment fully and enjoy it, and surrender the future to God. But focusing on the here and now is hard to do at times. I feel like I have to wear a helmet and live in a crash position for fear of life's next blow. That's how I've been going through life, constantly anxious about what's coming next, what unforeseen struggle will make things difficult all over again. Sometimes I want to go back and live at the clinic in Germany—I felt so safe there. But then I remind myself, that's where I found out about Farrah's cancer. Even the comfort of that place has been tainted by the power of uncertainty now.

*God, help me here. I'm struggling with trying to understand all this. I want my friend to be okay. I don't want to see her go through this painful experience and yet I can't stop it, just like I can't prevent my children from suffering. I don't know the answer, God. Maybe I just have to surrender it to you and trust that she will be okay, that*

*my kids are safe and protected, that I am as well. Let me*
*feel your loving presence, God, wherever you are, whatever*
*you are.*

*Thank you, God.*
*Amen*

◈ *October 12, 2006*

Tina and I went to see Farrah yesterday afternoon. I made
the minestrone soup and her favorite ginger cookies, and Tina
brought her a giant, I mean *giant,* teddy bear. It was bigger than
both of us. It barely fit into my car. Tina Sinatra is one of my oldest and very best friends and the godmother of my children. I
don't remember exactly when she and Farrah met, but we all became very close, the three of us, almost instantly. She was devastated when she heard about Farrah's cancer. Her other very close
friend Suzanne Pleshette was battling lung cancer, as well as our
mutual friend Freddie Fields. She had already experienced first-
hand the ravages of cancer. And now Farrah, too . . .

When we arrived at Farrah's apartment, Tina and I went into
her bedroom with the bear and waited for her to come out of the
bathroom. When she walked out, we couldn't believe it. She
looked radiant, a vision all in pink. Her skin was glowing and her
hair fell in soft waves around her face. You wouldn't have thought
anything was wrong with her if it weren't for the IV coming out
of her arm and the attached chemo pack, which administers the
chemo twenty-four hours a day.

Farrah was so happy we came. We ended up having a lot of laughs, all piled on the bed with that gigantic bear. We took silly pictures and gobbled up the ginger cookies . . . and then, of course, we finally got around to the elephant in the room. She told us in great detail about her cancer treatment. I tried to smile, to put on a stoic face, to act normal, but I still couldn't quite believe that my best friend had cancer. I just wanted to make it all go away for her; the pain, the discomfort, the fear she must be feeling. She's strong, but I know she has to be scared. If it were me, I would never be this brave. I'd be out of my mind with fear. But maybe once the shock has worn off, you're too busy walking through it to be afraid?

I went to a little Kabbalah memorial for Evelyn Ostin this morning. Evelyn was the wife of Mo Ostin, who was head of Warner Bros. Records for many years—and she was one of the most beloved women in town. I studied Kabbalah in a group that met at her house every week. It was the one-year anniversary of her death, and Rabbi Eitan Yardeni, who taught our Kabbalah classes, gave a very inspiring talk about gratitude and how important it is to feel fortunate in your life instead of feeling like a victim. It felt like he was speaking directly to me; it struck a nerve. "Focus on giving back to the world instead of focusing on yourself," he said.

Eitan said that our energy attracts situations into our lives and that the biggest disease we all have is selfishness. He said that "getting" will never make us feel fortunate, no matter how much we get, but that a spirit of gratitude will shift our energy and help us "get out of ourselves" and think about others more.

This is my biggest roadblock. I'm always in my head, focused on me or my kids, my personal world. I worry about the future—my future—and that worry can begin to consume me. I know I have to expand and get outside myself and find where I can really contribute my time and energy to help others. If I could just focus my brain! It always seems to be all over the place, like a wild horse that needs to be corralled.

### October 13, 2006

I went with Farrah to UCLA for her radiation and to get the line for the chemo removed. She'd been up all night, terribly sick and in pain. They had told her this would be the worst day, but she'd had no idea it would be this bad. At least she won't have any more chemo until the last week of radiation, so she has a four-week reprieve. I never realized that radiation causes so much pain; I thought it was the lesser of the two evils (chemo being the worst). I've never been this close to anyone who was going through cancer. It's such a hideous process—painful, debilitating, and un-relenting.

By the time we got back to Farrah's house, she was exhausted, but still managed to laugh and make a joke or two. Then she got serious and thanked me for taking her. "Sorry to have taken up so much of your time," she said.

"Are you kidding?" I said. "I wanted to do it."

I realized she's so much like me. I always worry that I'm putting friends out if they go out of their way for me. Farrah's always there for everyone else—whether it's her family, her friends, or people she's working with. Now she needs to let people be there for her.

## ❖ *October 16, 2006*

Farrah called from the hospital. They had to admit her because she had two blood clots from the IV line they had put into her arm. God, I can't believe my friend has to go through all this. It's ridiculous that the treatment itself is causing more problems for her. It makes me so angry.

## ❖ *November 2, 2006*

Farrah has about three more weeks of radiation left. The doctors warned her that she might want to quit because it gets so difficult, but *quit* is not a word in Farrah's vocabulary. She always seems to think people are exaggerating—that things can't ever be as bad as they'd have you believe. She's much more of an optimist than I am.

But she wasn't prepared for this; neither of us was. The radiation is brutal and torturous. They keep increasing the dose until she's up to about twenty-five minutes. That's shocking to me. Our friend, who had lung cancer, was getting six minutes at the peak of his treatment. The side effects are painful and debilitating. Sometimes all she can do is sob because it's so excruciating. And there's no end in sight. Three more weeks of this.

Every day I call to check on her and see if I can do anything for her, but after she gets her treatment (which she does every day), she just wants to sleep. I always offer to take her, but Ryan or her assistant, Mike, usually goes with her. Ever since her cancer was announced, the paparazzi have been stalking her. The doctor's office organized a way to get her into the building where she has her radiation. They go through the underground parking garage to a special door where they're met by Sheldon, from Dr. Gitnick's office, who escorts them to the radiation room. This usually gives those vultures the slip.

But one day, after she'd finished the radiation, she came out the door, and there sat an SUV with four paparazzi inside, videoing her and taking photos. Poor Sheldon watched frozen in surprise and disbelief as she walked right up and confronted them. She was exhausted and in pain, but her outrage gave her the strength to fight back.

"What is wrong with you people? Don't you have any respect for someone going through cancer treatment?" she asked angrily.

But the cameras kept clicking away; she was giving them quite a show. Then she tried to grab the guy's camera away from him and they struggled. "I couldn't get him to let go, so I swear, I punched him right in the arm as hard as I could!" she told me later. She took great pleasure in telling me the story. I know that if she'd had a knife on her, she would have slit his tires.

That's my feisty Texas friend!

"You go, girl!" I cheered as she told me the story. "The only thing I'm worried about is that the guy will slap you with an assault charge!"

"I don't care!" she said defiantly. "Let him. That'll look great. Harassing a woman when she's coming out of radiation. I'd love to see that one go to court!"

We laughed. Nothing—not paparazzi, not pain, not the promise of a long road ahead—was going to knock Farrah down.

### November 7, 2006

When I picked up the phone this morning, it was Farrah. For a minute I didn't recognize her voice: she was crying and her voice sounded tiny and weak.

"What's the matter, honey?" I asked, my heart jumping into my throat.

"I just feel so weak and so sick, and I'm in so much pain. I don't know how I can make it to radiation."

"I'm coming over right now," I said. I'd never heard her sound quite like this before—and it scared me. I was used to Farrah being strong. I knew that at this moment I had to be strong for her. I needed to be there for her just as I knew she would be there for me if the tables were turned.

"No, it's okay," she sobbed. "You don't have to. Mike can take me." Just like Farrah: she never wants to cause anyone any inconvenience.

"I'll be right there," I insisted. Fortunately, I can be stubborn, too. I threw on my clothes and drove as fast as I could to her apartment. I went upstairs and into her bedroom, where she was trying to pull on her Uggs. She was in so much pain from where the damned radiation had burned her that she could hardly walk. Her assistant, Mike, helped me get her down to her car. I got into the backseat with her, and he drove to the secret underground entrance, which was obviously no longer secret.

Sheldon, from the doctor's office, was waiting with a wheelchair. I looked around, making sure there were no paparazzi lurking about. The coast was clear. We went straight to the radiation room, where she lay down on the table for the treatment. It took about twenty minutes. Afterward we took her in the wheelchair back to the car and home, where I helped her back into bed. She winced with every step, but at least it was over. She'd made it for today.

"Just look at this," she said with a sigh, showing me the skin on the inside of her legs and her buttocks where they had radiated. I was shocked. It was bright red and blistered to the point that it was peeling off. It looked like a second-degree burn, and it was so excruciatingly painful, she could barely lie down. She'd been given salve and medication, but it wasn't even making a dent in the pain. It seems barbaric that this supposed cure is so ravaging.

I hope the doctors are right, that this will cure her cancer. After all this, they'd better be.


❧ *December 6, 2006*

The tabloids are out of control. They print anything they want, even if there's not a shred of truth to it. The *National Enquirer* has not let up on Farrah since she was diagnosed with cancer.

"You won't believe this headline," Farrah called to inform me today. She was furious. They had gone too far this time. It read, "Farrah Says: 'I Want to Die!'"

I know it's upsetting to her on many levels. First of all, her family and her friends read this garbage, and although most of us know it's not true, it still scares a lot of people who perhaps don't know how the tabloids lie and exaggerate.

"Can you ever hear me saying those words?" she fumed. "I get all these letters from people who are also battling cancer, and they're upset because they think I'm giving up. That's not encouraging them to keep fighting when they hear something like that. Don't these tabloids realize it's not just me they're hurting?"

Farrah can never figure out where they get these stories, since sometimes there are some accurate details involved. Someone has to be leaking information. But this headline goes way beyond an issue of privacy. It's becoming very clear to Farrah—and to me—that her cancer battle is not just about her anymore. People have always looked up to her—she's the golden girl, an American icon, the picture of beauty and vitality. But now they're looking to her for another reason: hope. And she'll be damned if she's going to let anyone— especially some vicious, lying tabloid—steal that hope away.

### Christmas 2006

Farrah finally finished her last week of radiation and chemo right after Thanksgiving. The holidays and several delays had made it run longer than planned. She was too sick to celebrate Thanksgiving, but we were hoping by Christmas she would feel more like herself. We have this tradition of making pies and cornbread stuffing on Christmas Eve.

But the radiation and chemo have taken a terrible toll on her. I had my usual Christmas dinner with my kids and a few close friends, but in the end she wasn't up to it. I promised her I'd make extra food and send some over, which I did. I always make the same down-home Texas Christmas dinner that my grandmother cooked when I was growing up—the food that Farrah and I both love. Farrah and I were very specific about our Texas food and how it had to be cooked: turkey with cornbread stuffing, mashed potatoes, sweet potatoes with marshmallows on top, creamed peas, brussels sprouts, giblet gravy, and, of course, our favorite pecan pie and coconut meringue pie.

The new year is approaching, and I always feel like it brings new hope—like you can wash away the past and start fresh. Farrah has high hopes for a full recovery, as the doctors have promised. I have high hopes that all of this will seem like a bad dream one day soon and our lives will be back to normal.

"Don't worry, honey," I told her. "Next year we'll be back in the kitchen, cooking up a storm together."

### February 2, 2007

I feel like the dark clouds have finally lifted. Farrah called me today: the doctors have declared her cancer free. Apparently the radiation and all that pain were worth it. We screamed our heads off on the phone—such joy! Such relief! The nightmare is finally behind her. Life can get back to normal.

There are so many things she's missed the last few months. We planned to have lunch and go shopping as soon as she was a little stronger—a girls' day out and a celebration of life.

## May 14, 2007

The last few months have been a relief—until today. Farrah's life was finally back to normal. She was getting back into her art (she's an amazing painter and sculptor), she was spending time with her loved ones, and she was making plans for the future.

And then today she went back to UCLA for her checkup. Everyone, including the doctors, was in shock: the cancer is back. It's the word she most dreaded hearing: *recurrence*. Ryan was supposed to take her in to meet with her doctors to hear what they felt the next step should be, but his car wouldn't start. So she grabbed her little handheld camera to help her remember all the information they were certain to throw at her, and took off to face it all by herself.

Her doctors want her to do this radical surgery that is horribly invasive and would mean part of her intestines would be removed and she'd have to wear a colostomy bag for the rest of her life. Understandably, she is not liking that prospect one bit. I arranged a conference call with her, me, and Dr. Ursula Jacob at the Leonardis Clinic in Germany. Farrah started to cry, and Dr. Jacob was sweet and reassuring.

"Don't cry, Farrah. You don't have to do this radical surgery. There is a great surgeon here who has a different way of removing the tumor that won't be as invasive and won't result in a colostomy. Then we will give you a special antibody treatment and build up your immune system to prevent the cancer from coming back."

Farrah felt much better after speaking with her, but she was

still confused. No wonder. The doctors in L.A. are being so adamant that theirs is the only way.

"What should I do?" Farrah asked me, uncertainty in her
voice. I understood; she was unsure about putting her life in the
hands of some foreign doctors she had never met. Meanwhile, the
doctors here were telling her that a very radical surgery was the only
way to save her life. "I don't know what to do," she said.

At this moment, I know, she was not thinking of only herself
but also of her family: How could she put her poor daddy through
this when he'd already lost Farrah's sister Diane to cancer in
2001? And Ryan: He is so attached to her. He can't bear to see her
suffer. Whereas I can be numb and emotionally detached when I
need to be, Ryan wears his heart on his sleeve. Then there's her
son, Redmond. "My sweet boy," she calls him. She worries about
him so. I know it's her son she's concerned about the most; she
wants him to have his mother for a long, long time.

I took a deep breath and thought hard before answering.
Then I said, "Honey, if it were me or my kids, I'd be on the first
plane to Germany." I meant it. I truly believe they can help her
there. From my stays at the clinic, I've seen how differently they
treat cancer than in the States, and how effective their methods
are. But I didn't want to make the decision for her. I didn't want to
be responsible—God forbid I should convince her to do it and it
ends up being a mistake.

"But," I added, "you have to make the decision yourself. Ask
God to show you the answer." After we hung up, I prayed for
God to guide her in the right direction, whether it was treatment
in America or in Germany. But in my heart, I felt strongly that
she should choose the latter. I find myself praying a lot these days;

in fact, I have for the last number of years. I've also pursued many spiritual teachings: Al-Anon, *A Course in Miracles,* Kabbalah, Science of Mind, and the writings of Marianne Williamson and Deepak Chopra. Pain, fear, and anxiety have made me dig deeper and keep searching for answers to give me more strength and comfort through difficult periods of my life.

❖ *May 18, 2007*

My birthday. Bren and Mel Simon threw me a big birthday party at their home in Bel Air tonight. It's been a hell of a week, and I wasn't feeling very festive. Farrah told me she really wanted to come and celebrate with me, but she didn't know if she was feeling up to it. Farrah is always wonderful at showing up for friends' birthdays or special events. In the years since we've been close friends, I don't think she's ever missed one of my birthdays or vice versa, unless one of us was out of town.

But this was different. The last thing she needed to do was to feel like she had to show up somewhere, especially with the whole world now knowing that her cancer had come back. People mean well, but the questions are so invasive, so draining: "How are you feeling? What do the doctors say? Are you *okay?*" I didn't want her to be subjected to all that.

"Please don't even think about it," I said. "As much as I love you, I never for a second thought you could make it. You're going through way too much."

The party was fabulous in every way; their house was beautiful, the food was amazing, and everyone was having a great time.

There were about sixty people seated in the party room downstairs, and dessert had just been served, when I looked up. There, walking into the room, were Farrah and Ryan, his arm protectively around her waist. This was the first time she'd been out to a party since she was diagnosed with cancer seven months ago. I was so shocked and so ecstatic to see them; I couldn't believe it. Farrah looked stunningly beautiful, almost ethereal, in a pale silver chiffon top and flowing pants. She was glowing; nothing about her said "cancer victim." The two of them could still stop traffic—forever the golden couple. The years hadn't diminished their charisma one bit.

I ran to Farrah and we hugged for a long time. Then she held out her arm and showed me the two beautiful matching bracelets she was wearing, one in platinum and one in rose gold. "I bought them today," she said. "I just thought . . . why not? I might as well treat myself." Then she took one off and gave it to me.

"This is your birthday present. If I die, you can have the other one, too," she joked, but I saw a hint of sadness behind her sweet smile.

"And if I die first, you can have mine back," I teased.

Her gesture touched me deeply. This was so like Farrah, to be going through this horrendous, life-threatening ordeal and still thinking about a birthday present for me. No matter what she was going through, she always thought about others.

Soon she was surrounded by everyone. It was always like that: people just flocked to her side. It didn't matter if it was a fan or a studio head, they were all equally in awe of Farrah. I watched her laughing, hugging friends and acquaintances, holding court. I was in awe of her, too, tonight.

*Celebrations with Farrah were always a party.*

*This photo was taken in 1988 on Farrah's birthday at Trader Vic's. We had a terrific time that night and drank a ton of Scorpions. But my memories of her are less about parties and more about the loyalty that she always showed to her friends.*

*A few months after this photo was taken, she was in the middle of filming a TV miniseries with Ryan called* Small Sacrifices *when I had a problem. I needed a paying acting gig to get my Screen Actors Guild health insurance reactivated. Without even blinking, Farrah called the producer, our friend Suzanne de Passe, and they gave me a part. There was this small scene involving Neighbor Number One and Neighbor Number Two; they were supposed to bring some food over to Farrah's character. Farrah made me Neighbor Number One. I just needed something with lines that would allow me to get my health insurance.*

Small Sacrifices *was filming in Edmonton, Canada. I arrived on the set and went into hair and makeup, where Farrah had them put me in this horrible polyester blouse, which stuck to me for every minute I was in the 100-degree heat. They sprayed my hair brown and pulled it back in a bun. They were trying to unglam me. Farrah loved it!*

*When I came out to film the scene, the director, a man named David Green, said to me, "Who are you, young lady?"*

*"Neighbor Number One," I answered.*

*"No you're not," he said. "You're Neighbor Number Two."*

*It turned out that he had hired someone else, and she had gotten my lines. Frantic, I found Farrah and reported that they'd cast someone else in my part. She immediately called Suzanne and straightened things out. I ended up playing Neighbor Number Two, but with a line written especially for me: "I brought you some potato salad . . ."*

*I got to keep my health insurance because of that potato salad . . . and Farrah. We laughed about Neighbor Number One and the polyester blouse for years.*

# TREATMENT IN GERMANY

❧ *May 20, 2007*

I called Farrah to tell her I'm going to leave for the Leonardis Clinic on Friday. I've had this trip planned for some time, so Sean can get his second round of treatments for ADD. I was hoping she would want to come with me. But there's a new development: the doctors at UCLA want to scan the rest of her body to see if the cancer has spread anywhere else. My heart stopped when she told me, but she was calm. The possibility of the cancer spreading beyond the tumor had never even occurred to me. She's having the scan on Thursday.

❧ *May 24, 2007*

The scan showed up something in her liver, but they have to do a biopsy tomorrow to find out if it's malignant. This is a nightmare. She's still calm but she's scared. So am I.

"I hate leaving on the day you're doing this," I said with a sigh.

"Don't worry," she assured me. "You go ahead. I'll call you as soon as I get the results. Who knows, I may be joining you."

## ❖ May 26, 2007

I arrived at the clinic today. Sean left two days before me so he's already here. I immediately told Dr. Jacob about Farrah's scan and the biopsy. By now, I knew, Farrah should have the results. Dr. Jacob told me she was certain it was cancer, and this was what she'd been afraid of from the outset: without the proper preventive treatment after the chemo and radiation, it will return.

Sure enough, I spoke to Farrah that night and it was cancer; there were a number of malignant tumors in her liver.

"It's a very aggressive, rare form," she said. Then that old determination fired up again. "I made up my mind. I'm coming to Germany. That's it." Then she asked tentatively, "Will you stay with me if I come?" I told her I would stay as long as she needed me.

I was so thankful she was coming here; I just knew they could help her. I hung up, and the reality of what was happening sank in: Farrah has cancer, and now it's metastasized to her liver. She could really die. I started crying. It was the first time I'd cried since she told me she had cancer. I let the tears run down my cheeks for several minutes. I let the pain and the fear wash over me. Enough, Alana. Be strong for her. Then that old familiar numb feeling came over me like a steel curtain drawn over my emotions. It's the way I've always dealt with shock or sadness or loss since I was old enough to remember. It's how I react when the pain is more than I can bear.

I pulled myself together and spoke to Dr. Jacob about what they could do. After we'd talked, I put her in touch with Farrah's doctor at UCLA so she could explain to him her ideas for treatment. She confirmed that this was a very serious, aggressive form of cancer and that the prognosis with standard chemo treatment would not be good. They had to figure out another way. While the oncologists at UCLA were still trying to come up with some choices, Farrah got on the plane with Ryan and her friend Joan Dangerfield. She came to Germany hoping she would find her miracle here.

### ❧ *May 30, 2007*

Farrah—along with Ryan and Joan—arrived today. I threw my arms around her and we both held on to each other for dear life, but we didn't have much time for catching up. Dr. Jacob arrived to meet Farrah for the first time. Farrah liked her immediately. It's hard *not* to like her, although she doesn't look anything like what one would expect of the head doctor of a German clinic. She's a large, buxom woman with short blondish-brown hair, and warm, compassionate eyes. She has a very outgoing, enthusiastic personality, and she was anxious to go over her ideas for Farrah's treatment plan, so we jumped right into it.

Ryan, Farrah, Dr. Jacob, and I gathered in Farrah's room, where Farrah handed me her little handheld camera and said, "Here. Will you film this so I can remember everything?"

"I don't know how to use this thing," I protested. "I'm lucky if I can use an Instamatic."

"It's so easy. You can do it. You're artistic," she joked. She showed me where the RECORD button was and basically how to point it in the right direction and I was off and running. She also took diligent notes and jotted down her questions. Neither one of us was going to miss a word.

Dr. Jacob had a lot to say, including that the prognosis for Farrah's kind of cancer at this stage was normally not good. Quiet tears slid down Farrah's cheeks, and Ryan asked the doctor, "Are we too late?"

"I'll never lie to you, Farrah," Dr. Jacob replied, "and I would be lying if I said I could guarantee you a cure . . ." We all held our breath. "But I have some ideas for a treatment plan and I think there is a very good possibility that it could work." We breathed a sigh of relief; at least there was hope here in Germany.

### *June 1, 2007*

Dr. Jacob didn't waste a minute; it was all moving quickly. Today I went with Farrah (Ryan and Joan stayed behind because there was no room in the van) and one of Dr. Jacob's team from the clinic to Frankfurt to meet Dr. Thomas Vogl, a much respected surgeon and radiologist and a professor at Goethe University. Farrah would be undergoing a procedure called chemo embolization, in which chemo is injected directly into the tumor to shrink it down to manageable size. It would later be removed by laser surgery. If there are multiple tumors in an organ, as there are in her liver, they use the same technique but "perfuse" the chemo throughout the organ—in essence, they bathe the liver in chemo. Although they're starting to do it in the States in trials, Dr. Vogl has been doing these procedures for over fifteen years and is known to be the master of them.

The waiting room and hallway outside his office were filled with people waiting to see him, but fortunately we were taken right in through a side door to where he was waiting for us. Dr. Vogl is a very tall, angular man with a balding head and glasses, attractive in a professorial sort of way. He is very precise, very detailed, and gets right to the point. I asked him if he would mind me filming the meeting, and I assumed that he would have a problem with it, but he was fine. These Germans are so different from doctors in the States! He explained briefly to Farrah what the procedure would be. She'd go right away for an MRI, come back to his office to go over the film, and then head straight into the operating room. Like I said, it all moves so quickly here.

Once Farrah had the MRI, Dr. Vogl brought us back into the office and put the film on the screen so we could see exactly where the tumors in her liver were. There they were: the invaders making my friend so ill.

We were escorted to the operating room, where Farrah put on a gown in a small adjoining cubicle and was taken by the nurse to the operating table. Of course, she was nervous. Who wouldn't be? But she still seemed fearless. I would have been freaking out. Here she is in a strange country with a doctor she's just met, getting ready to go through a procedure that she knows very little about. Her courage astounds me.

Dr. Vogl gave me permission to film the entire procedure,

which surprised me again. I put on a heavy lead apron that weighed a ton, because of the radiation that was emitted by the machines. Farrah had her rosary in her hand, clutching it to her heart, as they started the IV and pain medication. Dr. Vogl marched in and it began. They don't put you completely out, for some reason we could never quite understand. "I like to talk to my patients—who else would I talk to?" Dr. Vogl explained with his dry wit. Farrah went along with it, trying to be strong; I would have demanded they knock me out.

He gave her an injection of a local anesthetic in a very long needle, which, by Farrah's reaction, must have been painful. Then he took a scalpel and made an incision in the artery in her right groin. Blood actually spurted up into the air like a fountain. Ordinarily I would have fainted at the sight of that, but somehow being behind the camera buffered the effect. He inserted a small wire tube into her artery and manipulated it with a small machine all the way into the liver. There were four monitors above her, showing what was happening inside her body. I'd never seen anything like this before and it was fascinating. Then he took the syringes of chemo and injected them into the tube, which took them directly to the liver. He did the same thing with the primary tumor in the anal area, and before we knew it, he was done.

"That is it. It is over," he said. Then he pulled off his gloves and mask, and went immediately to his next procedure. Apparently he does fifteen to eighteen of these a day.

Farrah was sleeping lightly, so she wasn't in any pain, which I was thankful for, and we were taken to a recovery room nearby where she would sleep for a few hours. After four hours, if there was no bleeding, she could leave for the clinic. Unbelievable how quickly and efficiently it all was done. Dr. Vogl came in briefly just before her recovery time was up, checked her, said she was free to go, and told her he would see her again in three weeks.

We got into the van to drive us the five hours back to the clinic. We'd made a bed for Farrah in the backseat because she was still pretty groggy. A couple of hours later, I was starving so we stopped at a German roadside place to get something to eat. Farrah popped up immediately and noticed there was a Whata-burger inside. Who would have thought they'd have them in Germany? They're a southern staple, and I know how much Far-rah likes them, so of course she insisted on coming in and getting a giant hamburger, which she wolfed down, followed by her fa-vorite drink, a Coca-Cola. She likes her Cokes with lots of ice; she likes everything with lots of ice, and believe me, it's not easy to get ice in Germany.

We got back to the clinic at about midnight. Farrah was walk-ing without any problem, and not feeling bad at all. This wasn't going to beat her. We Texas girls are tougher than that.

### June 3, 2007

Farrah had her first antibody treatment today, which will fight the cancer and keep it from spreading during the procedure tomorrow. Ryan has been really sweet with her. Today, after the anti-allergy drip, she was so knocked out she just slept all day, and Ryan sat by her bedside, just watching her sleep. He wouldn't budge an inch . . . just in case she opened her eyes. He wanted her to know he was there.

❖ *June 4, 2007*

We're here at the hospital in Bad Tölz, a little town about twenty-five minutes away from the clinic. Farrah's gone into the operating room now with Dr. Jacob and the surgeon. They're going to use this special ultrasound procedure to remove the primary tumor, unless it's too deep in the muscle, in which case she will have to get a type of radiation that will go directly into the remains of the tumor and destroy it. She looked small and scared when she left the room on the gurney.

**Later**

Farrah's finally back in the room, but it was way more complicated than they thought. The tumor was much larger than it appeared in the PET scan or the reports from UCLA. Also, it was embedded in the muscle, very close to the vaginal wall. The surgery took much longer than expected, but they managed to get it all, they believe. The biopsy results will come back in a day or so to show if there are any cancer cells in the surrounding tissue. It just seems that with every step there's an unforeseen complication.

It's hard to see her in this kind of pain. After all she went through at UCLA, she said she didn't want to go through any more pain, but that just hasn't been possible. It all sounded easier and less complicated than it proved to be—the liver perfusion in Frankfurt, the ultrasound surgery. I can't bear to see her suffer.

Please, God, let this be the worst of it. I hope I've done the right thing by getting her to come here. What if I'm not right about this place? What if she doesn't get well? But they didn't have anything to offer at home, and here they are doing things that are only in trials in the United States, if even that. At least there's hope here.

◈ *June 5, 2007*

We're back at the clinic now. The biopsy came back and they got all the cancer in the surgery! Thank you, God! We were so excited when Dr. Jacob told us. We were all jumping up and down, and Dr. Jacob even started crying. This was such a huge victory. Farrah's still in pain from the surgery, but we all went for a walk to the beautiful little church in the village. I think we all wanted to thank God in person! The church was first built in the 1200s, then obviously refurbished at different times. We were awestruck by its beauty and magnificence. The ceiling was painted with powerful images of saints and angels almost as impressive as the artwork in the Sistine Chapel. We never expected to find something like this in the middle of this tiny village of Bad Heilbrunn.

Farrah knelt in one of the pews and prayed. She said the words silently, although I could see her lips moving. I know she felt very grateful for the good news she'd just had and wanted to thank God. Raised a Catholic, she has a very strong faith and prays often; she even crosses herself or says grace before every meal. I was filming this lovely moment, but somehow I ended up erasing the film. I probably wasn't supposed to be filming in the church anyway.

That night we celebrated. Ryan, Farrah, and I curled up on her bed, ate spaghetti Bolognese—one of the few dishes Farrah liked at the clinic—and watched movies. Ryan had wanted to see some strange French art film with subtitles, but I insisted on lighter fare: *Meet the Fockers*. We needed something to lift our spirits and take our minds off the seriousness of this trip.

*June 14, 2007*

I'm having such an anxiety attack. My son Sean just got back to L.A. and found out the cops are issuing a warrant for his arrest over an altercation he was involved in. They've charged him with assault and battery along with several other things. It was actually one of his friends who started the whole fight, not him. Sean was the one who got singled out because he was more high profile. And Sean won't rat out his friend, so he's taking the rap for it. I'm frantically trying to find an attorney for him. This was another thing that Farrah and I could spend hours talking about: our boys. We never dreamed that one day we'd have this in common.

I was with Farrah and Dr. Jacob when Farrah got her first chemo treatment. Dr. Jacob explained that she'll have the chemo once a week, and they mix it with liposomes to get into the cancer cells easier. At the same time, they do a local hypothermia (freezing) of the liver to destroy the cancer. At the end of next week she goes to Frankfurt for another liver perfusion and maybe the laser surgery. Tomorrow she gets a special injection that we hope will genetically rearrange the RNA of the cancer cells and cause them to die.

### June 16, 2007

This past week has been crazy: Sean's arrest, my frantic attempts to find an attorney for him, all the drama around Farrah, and now this situation with George. He's here at the clinic for his annual checkup; he goes to the clinic like other people go for a facial.

This doctor from Düsseldorf arrived who has been treating him for his knees and shoulder. Farrah and I jokingly refer to her as "the stripper doctor" because she's blond, curvaceous, and not at all what you'd expect a doctor to look like. She arrived to treat different people at the clinic and moved right into George's room (next door to me, by the way, which I think is a little indiscreet). Suddenly I realized that the doctor is sleeping with George, a fact that he neglected to tell me. I know that George and I don't have a romantic relationship anymore—it's been over thirty years since we divorced—but we are close and, in some way, still very connected. I would never do something so insensitive to him.

And my ex Rod Stewart's getting married again. I suppose he'll be having more children; he collects them like he does Galle lamps. I'd never want to be with him again, that's for sure, but it's just that everyone seems to be able to find new relationships and move on with their lives except me. I feel overwhelmed with my children's problems (even though they're grown), my best friend's cancer, and my own fears of the future. I'm uncertain about how I'm going to survive physically, emotionally, and financially.

### June 23, 2007

Yesterday, Farrah had to go to Frankfurt for her second chemo perfusion, and Ryan decided that he would take her. He knew she'd had a relatively easy time with the procedure the first time we'd gone, so he anticipated it being a piece of cake. Farrah was a little nervous about him accompanying her, since I was the one who knew the routine. But beyond that, I know Farrah didn't want to have to worry about Ryan worrying about her.

"Don't you want Alana to come, too?" she asked him tentatively.

"No, it's okay. I can handle it," Ryan replied in a very manly, take-charge kind of way. Famous last words.

I only found out what happened this morning when I woke up. Dr. Jacob said Farrah was up all night sick from the chemo they put in the liver perfusion in Frankfurt. The procedure with Dr. Vogl had gone well, and after she'd spent a few hours in the recovery room, they got into the van to head back to the clinic. She started throwing up shortly after they left Frankfurt and continued for the entire six hours that it took to get back to the clinic.

They had to keep stopping by the roadside because all the containers kept filling up. Even the doctor from the clinic, who accompanied them, was at a loss for what to do. Nothing seemed to work. She threw up until the wee hours of the morning, when finally she fell into an exhausted sleep. The good news is that the tumors have shrunk considerably, though still not enough to do the laser surgery on this trip.

I went in to see Farrah around noon, when the nurse said she was finally awake. She was feeling weak and shaky, which was to be expected. Then Ryan came into the room with a bacon sandwich he'd brought her from the dining room. He was so proud of himself. A bacon sandwich! We laughed the rest of the trip about Ryan's choice of food for her still delicate stomach. Such a typical man!

There are so many different energies going on here: Redmond, Farrah and Ryan's son, arrived a few days ago with Mel and Bren Simon on their plane; my daughter, Kimberly, flew in from London; Ryan; Joan; George and his girlfriend, Barbara—I can't call her "the stripper doctor" anymore because she's actually very nice. And she did a little Botox and filler on me yesterday. It's kind of made up for her sleeping with my ex-husband. I'm not sleeping with him, so I guess he has to sleep with someone eventually or be a monk. It might as well be someone who's nice (and who does wonders with Botox). She didn't even charge me. Yes, I can be bought.

As for my lips, I can't quite decide if they're great or not. I asked Farrah if they're too big. "No, Mick, they're not too big," she quipped.

◈ *July 1, 2007*

Home again! I can't believe June is over and I have spent the entire month at the clinic. Now it's back to reality and what comes with it—uncertainty. I'm nervous about Sean's hearing on Tuesday—the arraignment. And Farrah. I know I just got unpacked, but I have this sudden impulse to run away back to Germany and that lovely, peaceful little village.

On our first trip to the Leonardis Clinic, it was just about summer when we arrived in late May. In the morning you'd open your windows and you could hear the cows softly mooing and smell the sweet scent of newly mowed hay. The scenery was almost too perfect, like something from The Sound of Music.

On one of the days when Farrah was feeling pretty good, we took a long walk through the picturesque countryside. Everything was lush and in bloom, and the ground was covered in a layer of fresh green. I thought that if ever there was a place and a time to get well, surely it was here.

We found some horses, and Farrah kept talking about "what a big ass" one horse had, which made us both laugh no end. The funniest thing was that she was right: it truly was the biggest ass you've ever seen! We decided we'd take a picture and make a card of it, and send it to anyone we knew who was a horse's ass (the list was endless!).

Then Farrah spotted this sweet baby horse lounging with his parents by an old farmhouse. She petted his mane and fed him; she whispered a few gentle words in his ear. After a few minutes she turned around and walked toward me, and together we headed back in the direction of the clinic.

# FIGHTING THE TERRORIST

---

❧ *September 9, 2007*

Farrah and I left Los Angeles tonight for Frankfurt and her next visit with Dr. Vogl. When we left Germany at the end of June, Dr. Jacob had said Farrah needed to come back in about two months. The tumors in her liver that Dr. Vogl had treated with the chemo perfusions might be small enough for him to perform the laser surgery to burn them out.

I haven't been feeling well the last couple of weeks myself. I think it's probably due to stress and anxiety about leaving again for a long trip. I had to cancel a trip back to Houston, where I was supposed to be the guest of honor and featured speaker at the fiftieth anniversary celebration of the high school that I graduated from, Stephen F. Austin. I felt it was quite an honor that they had asked me, considering that Mrs. LeGros, the dean when I was a rather rebellious senior there, had once said that I would never amount to anything more than a carhop (well, I was a stewardess for a while!). I had also made plans to visit my eighty-five-year-old uncle in Nacogdoches, Texas, my hometown, and I was feeling terribly guilty about disappointing him. But this trip is about trying to save my friend's life, so it has to take priority.

### *September 10, 2007*

We landed and came straight to the hospital to meet with Dr. Vogl about Farrah's surgery tomorrow. She had an MRI, and afterward he showed us what size the tumors were now and which ones he would laser. Some of them were already dead or dying from the chemo treatment she'd had on the last trip. Farrah wanted to know why he couldn't laser all of them, but he said that it was dangerous to do too many at one time. It can cause severe bleeding. That was so typical of Farrah. She didn't want to mess around; she wanted to face them head-on and burn the suckers out. All of them!

Afterward we went to check into the hotel, a small, modern structure with colored neon lights in the lobby. We dubbed it "the disco hotel." We ate, showered, and went to bed, exhausted from the long trip and our afternoon with Dr. Vogl.

### *September 11, 2007*

I'm lying on the other bed in Farrah's hospital room, watching her sleep. We've been here all day and I'm dying to go back to the hotel and shower and eat, but I don't want to leave her until the private nurse gets here. God, she's had the day from hell. We arrived at the hospital around nine and they began preparing her for the laser surgery. I was nervous because Dana, my astrologer, had said they mustn't do the surgery between 10 A.M. and 2 P.M. She said that if they did it during those hours, it might have to be repeated. Farrah has probably never consulted an astrologer in her life, but she knows I put a lot of stock into it, so she goes along with it. Especially about something like this.

I told Dr. Vogl what the astrologer said, but I prefaced it by saying that I knew he would think I was a crazy American. Dr. Vogl is very rigid and Germanic, but now that we know him better, Farrah and I both get a kick out of giving him big hugs when we see him. I think we enjoy it because he receives our hugs with a kind of embarrassed stiffness, patting us on the backs like an uncomfortable father. Farrah thinks he likes me because I always flirt with him a little so he'll let me film.

He promised they'd be through by ten, but I have my doubts. The first part of the laser procedure ended up being excruciatingly painful. Dr. Vogl didn't tell Farrah about this part. She was given pain medication by IV but was not out completely, and they inserted these thin metal skewers, for want of a better word, that were about eighteen inches long, through her skin and her rib cage into her liver. The pain was almost unbearable for her. I had been filming it, but I had to stop and go to the anesthesiologist. I demanded they give her something stronger to knock her out. This guy looked like an SS officer and spoke with a German accent that was right out of a *Saturday Night Live* skit.

"We cannot do that. She must be awake so she can breathe when Dr. Vogl says. The instruments must be inserted very precisely." Then, with a sadistic little smile, he said, "Dr. Vogl is the master of the puncture!"

"This is inhuman. You can't let her be in this kind of pain. Can't you give her stronger pain medication?" I pleaded.

"I will give her something more," he relented. Then he explained, "When she goes into the other room for the laser surgery, she will be completely out." Well, thank God for some mercy.

I couldn't film the actual laser surgery because they said it would destroy the tape in the camera, so I waited outside. Dr. Jacob had just arrived, so we went to see Farrah in the recovery room when she came out, still under the anesthesia. Dr. Vogl came out and said that he had removed one tumor close to the wall of the liver, two small inactive ones on the left lobe, and one larger one. There was another tumor that was still too large and too close to a blood vessel to laser, so he wanted to wait a couple of hours and then do a chemo embolization and perfusion to further shrink the tumor.

Unfortunately, Farrah will need to have another laser surgery in a few weeks. I can't believe what she's been through this year. Nobody deserves to have to suffer like this. But somehow she manages to retain her sense of humor. Later, when Dr. Vogl came into the room to see her, she asked him if she could have a set of the "skewers" that he uses to puncture the liver. She said she wanted them so she could practice on other people! He smiled. By now he's getting used to her sense of humor.

Dr. Vogl examined her briefly, declared the laser surgery a success, and swept out of the room without further conversation. Farrah nicknamed him "Dr. In and Out."

❧ *September 12, 2007*

We were picked up by Dr. Jacob's driver and began the five-hour drive to the new clinic where Dr. Jacob has moved her practice.

It's in a little town called Bad Wiessee on Lake Tegernsee, one of the most beautiful areas in Bavaria. Each of the surrounding towns and villages is right on the lake, surrounded by the Bavarian Alps. It's quite breathtaking. We arrived at the Alpenpark, the new clinic, and were taken to our rooms, which were up two flights of stairs. No elevator in sight. But they had a beautiful view overlooking the lake and the mountains. The clinic itself was very different from the Leonardis, which I loved because it was small and the service was very personal. This clinic was a large, sprawling facility that treated mostly older German patients recovering from orthopedic surgeries and needing rehabilitation. Dr. Jacob had rented a small area of the clinic for her practice. It felt big and impersonal and slightly confusing, and the hallways at night had an eerie feeling. The first night I told Farrah I felt like we were in *The Shining*. I expected Jack Nicholson to leap out of one of the rooms with a knife. Here we were again, beginning a brand-new chapter in our adventure.

### September 20, 2007

I went to sleep while Sean's preliminary hearing was still going on back home. This would determine whether his case would go to trial, and I checked my e-mail for the results the minute I woke up. I was disappointed to learn that the judge hadn't thrown the case out but had sent it to trial, which will take place in a few months. I was pretty upset, but I couldn't reach anyone until later because it was the middle of the night in L.A. Then Farrah and I had to leave the clinic to go to Frankfurt on our friends Bren and Mel Simon's plane, which they very kindly gave us for the day. Farrah was to have the final tumor in her liver lasered, unless it hadn't shrunk enough, in which case Dr. Vogl would do another embolization.

We got off to a rocky start when the driver waiting for us outside the clinic pointed out two paparazzi hiding in the bushes. Apparently the groundskeeper of the clinic had just chased one with a pitchfork. Way to go! I made Farrah stay inside while the car went around to the back entrance. I tried to photograph the paparazzi with my camera, but they slunk away deeper into the woods. We got to the plane (a beautiful G5), took off, and landed in Frankfurt without incident. But when we arrived at Dr. Vogl's clinic there was another paparazzo waiting, and he got a picture before we realized what was happening.

Then, when we arrived in Dr. Vogl's office, he explained that he couldn't laser the tumor because it was too soon after the other laser treatment. "It could be dangerous," he said. "So I will embolize it." Farrah was surprised and quite disappointed because she'd hoped he was going to do the laser treatment and then the tumors would all be gone.

She was really nervous and crying a little when they put her on the operating table, but by the time the IV started to take effect, she was chatting and joking with Dr. Vogl as he performed the intricate procedure. I've never seen anything quite like it. This man is a true scientific genius. He let me stay in the operating room filming it, as I'd done before. I know I've said it before, but they would never allow this in the States.

Afterward, when the drugs started wearing off, Farrah started complaining of pain in her liver. They gave her some pain drops and nausea drops orally in water, which I knew was a mistake. I even questioned the doctor before he gave them to her, warning him, "She tends to get very nauseated after any procedure and can start vomiting violently."

Did he pay any attention to me? Of course not; he's German.

So, about thirty minutes later, when I was in the anteroom talking to Dr. Jacob on the phone, I heard this splashing noise, then another, and another. I rushed into the room to see Farrah projectile vomiting. "Oh God," I said to Dr. Jacob. "She's throwing up!" The last time it happened after this procedure was the time Ryan was with her, and she threw up for over eight hours nonstop. I told the doctor who had given her the drops that she must have the medication *immediately* to stop the vomiting, but it had to be given by IV, not orally. The oral meds would take too long to work.

Nothing they gave her had any effect at all. It would look like she was nodding off, and then suddenly she'd start throwing up all over again. She was almost totally knocked out from all the drugs they'd given her, but still nothing stopped the vomiting. Dr. Vogl kept coming in, checking on her, and scratching his head. It was the first time I'd ever seen him at a loss for what to do.

"You think you can still make the plane?" he asked. She kept mumbling, "Yes, I want to go," in between bouts of heaving.

He shrugged and then turned to me: "Well, she seems to want to go."

Okay, now I was pissed. Who was the doctor here?

"She just threw up again five seconds ago," I said. "Do you really think she's capable of making that decision?"

"Well, you're her friend. You know her. Do you think she can go?"

I hate when people answer a question with a question. I said, "Look, I'm not a doctor, how can I know if she's able to go?" This was getting ridiculous. There was no way she could travel—back me up on this, will you, Doc?

Finally, after it was apparent that nothing was going to stop her violent vomiting, even she realized there was no way we were getting on that plane. I called the pilots and explained what had happened and how sorry I was. They called Bren Simon, and she told them to spend the night and bring us back the next day. God bless her. A five-hour ride in a bouncing van would have been a nightmare. Unfortunately for us, the nightmare was just beginning.

This was a day clinic, where people don't spend the night, but we had no choice—we weren't going anywhere. So Dr. Vogl arranged for a small room with two beds and his private nurse to stay with us. When we got to the room, it was around 9 P.M., and Farrah continued to throw up. They kept giving her more and more medication, and I was getting more concerned by the moment. I kept calling the doctor, asking what was causing such a violent reaction, and he said it was the chemo.

"I had to give her a very aggressive dose in order to kill this terrorist," he explained. He always referred to the cancer as a terrorist. "Some people do have this kind of reaction." Thanks for telling us now. Just when the medication seemed to be taking effect and

Farrah would doze off, the next moment she'd be reaching for the barf box (for lack of the technical term). She threw up about seventy-five times altogether (she told me the next day that she'd kept an accurate tally).

After a bit, I sneaked out into the hallway to eat the pizza and spaghetti Bolognese I'd had delivered before all this started. Who would have thought that I of the squeamish stomach could actually wolf down a pizza while my best friend was throwing up in the next room? But I was starving.

Then, in the middle of all this, Sean called, very upset about the outcome of his hearing. My nerves were raw. We argued and he hung up on me. I was upset and called Dana Cole, his attorney, to try to make some sense of what was happening. He said it wasn't as bad as Sean thought it was, that very few cases got thrown out in the preliminary, and that the other side didn't have a strong case at all and we did. I felt slightly better and somewhat relieved, but still, every time I thought about it I felt weak in the knees. After all, he is still my baby boy.

Luckily, I'd brought a pair of pajamas in my carry-on case and even found my eye mask from the flight over, so I brushed my teeth and crawled into the tiny bed next to Farrah's. I turned out the lights hoping for the best, but no such luck. Every time I'd hear her reach for the throw-up pan, I shot up in bed, turned on the light, and went to get the nurse. The poor nurse didn't speak English and just kept throwing her hands up to the sky and saying, "Mein Gott! Mein Gott!" Pleading for God to intervene didn't seem to be working. She was kind of crazy and very melodramatic. Farrah looked at me between sieges of vomiting and said, "Oh God, they've sent me a loon!" From that moment on, we officially called her "the loon," and couldn't stop laughing when she walked into the room. We always managed to find the humor, even in the most harrowing situations. All my life I practically fainted at the sight of blood or even a hangnail. And here I am holding Farrah's head as she throws up and wiping her face. This gives a whole new meaning to friendship for me.

There wasn't much I could do for Farrah except call the loon and try to make sure she was warm enough and as comfortable as possible under the circumstances. Finally, around 4 A.M., she fell into a deep sleep. Thank God, I thought it would never happen. I went to sleep as well, after taking two Ativan. I'd told the nurse on duty not to let anyone wake us under any circumstances; we both needed to sleep. She said Dr. Vogl usually came in at five thirty.

"Is he crazy?" I snapped at her. "Tell him I said that if he wakes us up, he's risking his life. You got that?"

I'm not sure she understood what I was threatening, but I must have looked like I meant it. She was intimidated enough to leave us sleeping until eight thirty, when the orderly came in to take Farrah for an MRI.

Farrah was a wreck, poor thing, but at least the vomiting had stopped. I was holding my breath, hoping that it didn't start again. We went for the MRI, where a mean technician yelled at me and wouldn't let me film her. Funny that Dr. Vogl, the god of all doctors, let me film everything, but this woman ordered me out. I was cranky enough already from lack of sleep and I was about to get into it with her but decided to let it slide. Pick your battles.

Dr. Vogl came into the room afterward and said that the tumor had been destroyed by this second embolization and that Farrah was now free of any active tumors.

"It's worth all you went through last night to have such a good result, yes?" he said.

That was for sure, we both agreed, and hopefully she'll never have to go through such a horrible experience again.

After that, everything went smoothly. We were picked up by the driver, went straight to the waiting plane, and were even able to take off two hours earlier than the time slot they had given us in the tower. We arrived in Munich and got into the waiting van, and Farrah slept for the hour's trip back to the clinic, as usual. Her eyes close the minute she gets into anything that moves. (I wish I could be so lucky.)

For years I've been trying to get Farrah to go on a road trip to Texas with me, just the two of us going back home. Whenever I bring up the idea, she always answers, "Why would you want me? You know I would just get in the car and go right to sleep and you'd be driving the whole way by yourself." I guess the only way to keep her awake would be to keep stopping for Mexican food. That would do the trick.

◈ *September 21, 2007*

Farrah and I went outside and sat in the sun. Well, I sat in the shade, and she sat in the sun. At times in my life when I've felt terribly overwhelmed and anxious, I've envisioned having one of those old-fashioned southern nervous breakdowns that my mother was always having, and going to one of those sanitariums where people in the South used to go. Farrah and I used to joke about it; we would say what a nice rest it would be, to sit in our lawn chairs with blankets over our legs, staring blankly out over the green, rolling hills. It hit me while we were sitting outside today that this place fits that picture to a tee. I guess you have to be really careful what you wish for.

We're quite a pair. People always think we're sisters because we look alike—it must be the hair. "Yeah, she's the older sister," I'd always say whenever they'd ask (never mind that I'm a couple of years older).

"Yeah, Alana gets younger every year," Farrah would tease back.

I'd try to convince her that she needed to lie about her age, but she'd always resist the urge.

"Why bother?" she'd say. "It always says, 'Farrah Fawcett, comma, insert age here,' when they write about me."

I'd smile, but then I'd see her name in print and she'd always be right.

*She always was a Texas girl.*

*In October 2007, Farrah and I went to Texas, after the second trip to Germany in September. We were there for her dad's ninetieth birthday, which was where this picture was taken. We stayed with him and his second wife, Sophie, for three or four days. Farrah gave him this sweater, and he was so happy that she had come home.*

*After a few days with her dad, we headed for Nacogdoches, my hometown, to see my Uncle Gene. Farrah wasn't feeling great, but she was determined to be a trouper; she didn't want to let me down. She was probably the only friend I've ever had whom I could always enjoy Texas with, who understood what it meant to be home. We had the most fun on that road trip—just two Texas girls cruising around the back roads, miles and lifetimes away from Germany and everything from the last year. We kept joking that we were Thelma and Louise without the .38.*

*All along our drive, we'd stop in these little dive restaurants, and the college girl waitresses would say to Farrah, "Does anyone ever tell you you look like that actress from* Charlie's Angels?"

*She'd smile and reply, "Yeah, sometimes . . ."*

*We stopped at Johnson's Café in Corrigan, Texas. We had heard they cooked a hot lunch buffet with chicken-fried steak, turnip greens, and black-eyed peas, and our mouths were watering. We were in hog heaven. The owner, a man named Dooley, said that if we let him know when we were coming back through, he'd cook us up some chicken and dumplings (my personal favorite) and some pies. We kept to our word, and so did he—and he made us lemon and coconut meringue pies to take home with us.*

*We spent the night in this motel and we had little adjoining rooms. Farrah went into her room and there was this huge bug in the bed. So after trying to oust it unsuccessfully, with much screaming and giggling, she came into my room and slept there instead. We were crazy, silly, and loving every minute of being Texas girls once more.*

# A PLEASANT DISTRACTION

It was a beautiful day again, and we sat outside in the afternoon and read. Today kind of reminded me of those wonderful weekends when we were younger and we'd occasionally escape to Ryan's beach house in Malibu. My kids would spend the weekend with their respective dads while Ryan would take care of Redmond at their house in town. Meanwhile, Farrah and I would run away for a couple of days of rest and recuperation from our busy schedules.

Just sitting in the sun and doing nothing was the most restful, healing medicine in the world. We'd bring a stack of fashion magazines and pore over them, comparing the things we found that we liked. We'd splurge and have the manicurist come down and do our nails and toes, or sometimes have a massage. If we felt like getting dressed and putting on makeup, which we usually didn't, we'd occasionally go to dinner at the little Italian restaurant in the Malibu Country Mart or even to the mediocre Mexican restaurant on Zuma Beach. By the end of the weekend, we'd be ready to go home and resume our lives.

Today felt like that. It was a great time; two girlfriends hanging out together just like it used to be.

I'm so glad we didn't leave today, even though we could have flown with the Simons on their plane. They would have gotten off in Indianapolis and sent us on to Los Angeles on the plane, which was incredibly generous of them, but Dr. Jacob felt Farrah wasn't ready to travel yet. I agreed with her, but it was awfully tempting.

Tonight Dr. Jacob wanted to take us down to this Italian restaurant, Mimmo's, which is supposed to be the best Italian food in the area and is practically across the street from the clinic. I got ready at the last minute and just threw on jeans with hardly any makeup, hoping to eat, get back to the clinic, and get into bed as soon as possible. It was a very charming, candle-lit restaurant, filled with attractive local people. It had the feel of a trattoria somewhere in the Italian countryside.

We were in the middle of our first course when the owner/ chef, Mimmo, came out to say hello to us. *Hello, indeed*. He was the cutest thing I'd seen in a long time, and certainly anywhere in Germany. Blond, blue-eyed, and *gorgeous*. He didn't speak a word of English, but I managed to remember a little of my Italian, which duly impressed him. We were flirting with each other in Italian.

The minute he left the table, Farrah started doing these wicked impersonations of me, batting her eyelashes and mocking my lame Italian. We were laughing so hard. Mimmo kept coming back to the table and ended up ordering a round of after-dinner drinks and joining us.

Meanwhile, the restaurant had gotten quite warm and Farrah took off her sweater, leaving her thin T-shirt underneath.

"Are you trying to steal my man?" I teased. "Show-off!"

But Mimmo (probably because of my lame Italian) seemed quite taken with me. He was making plans to come to Los Angeles in November. He told us he was forty, which surprised me. I'd thought he was in his late twenties, so I was relieved not to be cradle-robbing. I was hoping he thought I was a lot younger than I am as well.

We finally said goodnight—Farrah practically had to pull me out of there because I was having so much fun, and she was having a great time making fun of me. Farrah liked Mimmo; she thought he was cute and sweet and he'd be good for me. Crazy. I came to Germany to help my friend fight cancer, and I might just have found a little romance.


*September 25, 2007*


Today was not such a good day. Farrah felt terrible, and so did I. I think it might have had something to do with the drinking last night. We were supposed to go back to Mimmo's tonight with Dr. Jacob and Farrah's good friends the Van Pattens, who had just arrived. But neither one of us felt like going. Farrah decided at the last minute that she really should go because she had told them she would. Farrah always tries to keep her commitments—even if she's feeling under the weather. So we got ourselves together, and off we went.

I put in a little more effort than last night, since Mimmo would be there. He was thrilled to see us, and brought us all sorts of wonderful pastas to try. By the end of the evening he was affirming that he was definitely coming to Los Angeles to see me in *"Noviembre."* I just kept laughing, batting my eyelashes, and saying *"Va bene."* When we got outside, I said, "I wonder where he intends to stay?"

Dr. Jacob looked at me in amazement and said, "With *you,* Alana!" As if to say, "It's pretty obvious, you nitwit."

Yikes! What if he is serious? What will I do with a gorgeous Italian chef who doesn't speak a word of English? And will he look as gorgeous when he arrives in L.A., probably in bad shoes and the wrong jeans? Guys sometimes just don't seem as attractive out of their native environment. I guess I'll cross that bridge when I come to it.

◈ *September 26, 2007*

We're on the plane on the way to Los Angeles. We just had a great meal with great service. Farrah is fast asleep and I was meditating when I had this great idea for a movie, inspired by Farrah talking about *Enchanted April,* which I've never seen but I think is about four older English women who go off to Italy to escape their mundane lives.

So here's my idea: A few girls rent a house in Italy for a month and just hang out. I could see it as a movie, or even a reality show. If we did it as a movie, maybe Cher would want to direct it. I don't know exactly what the plot would be, but it would involve four single California women. One of them would be the Farrah character, who is recovering from cancer. One would be my character, who is worried about her financial future and looking for an Italian billionaire (millionaires just don't meet the criteria anymore). She, of course, falls in love with an Italian chef. Then there could be one woman who is recovering from a terrible state of depression, and another who has just found her husband in bed with another woman (or maybe even another man!). Anyway, there are lots of possibilities, but I'm not sure where I go from here. And do I need a younger woman (or two) in this plot? I don't know how easy it would be to get any movie made with four women over fifty. That's just reality in Hollywood.

Anyway, that's my idea for now. I always have great ideas, but I'm never quite sure how to carry them out. I can't make a decision, so I go around in circles and ultimately do nothing. I wish I could be more like Farrah in this respect; she's a risk taker and doesn't waste time once she puts her mind to something. She has a saying that she loves: "Life is sweetened by risk." She even named her production company Sweetened By Risk.

◈ *November 11, 2007*

I haven't written for a while, even though I've been back from Germany for a month and a half. So much on my mind. The first thing I have to face is that Mimmo is definitely coming in a week, and I'm slightly panicked. It was all fun and laughs when we discussed it in Bad Wiessee. But truthfully, I never thought he would *really* come. He e-mailed me the minute I got home that he had booked his ticket. Suddenly reality hit: What the hell was I thinking? This man whom I hardly know is coming to stay at my house! What if he's some pervert or an ax murderer?

I called Dr. Jacob to see how well she knew him, and I was relieved when she told me she's known him for a few years and that he's a very decent, nice, hardworking guy. The fact remains that I don't know what he's expecting. A romance? Or just a nice trip to Los Angeles, where he's never been? I've decided he can stay here, in the guest room, I can show him around L.A., and we can be friends. I'll make that very clear, so that hopefully there will be no problem of him having other expectations.

I also don't want to build up any expectations on my part of what it might be. I don't want to jump into anything too quickly and then regret it. If I behave responsibly, I won't have to face that kind of uncomfortable situation, right? Marianne Williamson said that I should only ask God that this be a blessing. That's a spiritual way to look at it, and it relieves me of trying to figure it out and be anxious about the outcome. It won't be uncomfortable if I'm just open and can be kind, be sharing, and enjoy it—even if the end result is only that I'm learning to speak Italian really well.

I spoke to Farrah about it several times; each time I was more panicked. She thought it was great that he was coming. But then she's not an anxiety-filled worrywart like me. She has a much simpler way of looking at things. She sees things more in the moment, not as a catastrophe-in-the-making.

"Oh, what could be bad?" she said. "He's gorgeous, he's sweet, and most importantly, he's a great cook! Have him cook for you *all* the time. For all of us!"

She's so practical about these things. Maybe she's right and I should just relax and focus on the present.

◈ *November 18, 2007*

Mimmo arrived. I went to the wrong terminal at the airport and ended up being an hour late picking him up. He was left standing in the international terminal alone, with no idea of how to reach me or where to go. I felt terrible. What a way to start his trip. But I apologized profusely, as much as I could in Italian, and he wasn't upset at all.

When I first saw him, he wasn't quite as gorgeous as he was that night in the restaurant. Hmm, it did have great lighting . . . He was a little shorter, maybe, than I remembered. I checked out the jeans and the shoes. They were at least not embarrassing, and God knows, we can certainly get him a great pair of jeans in L.A. I've been taking a few Italian lessons, so by now I can speak enough to have a conversation, which I had rehearsed with my teacher: "How was your flight?" "Did you sleep on the plane?" "Are you hungry?"

We arrived at my house. What immediately impressed me was how much my dogs took to him and vice versa. Lolita, my big French Mastiff and the love of my life (other than my kids), was all over him, and Bliss, my long-haired Chihuahua who I inherited from Kim when she moved to London, and who doesn't usually like men at all, was right up in his lap. He nicknamed her "Principessa." I showed him to his room and asked if he was hungry, and he said he'd like to eat something, so I took him to Il Sole, a lovely little Italian restaurant on Sunset. We chatted, finished a very good dinner, although not as good as his cooking, and went back to my house. We both retired for the night, I to my room and he to the guest room. I breathed a sigh of relief. Perhaps this wasn't going to be so uncomfortable after all.

My only big worry now is that I've realized that Thanksgiving falls right in the middle of his visit. How do I explain this strange Italian man to my kids when they come for our traditional Thanksgiving dinner? I begged Farrah to come with Ryan and Redmond so I don't have to face this on my own.

❧ *November 19, 2007*

We were hit with unexpected news today. I went with Farrah and Ryan for her scan at Dr. Lawrence Piro's office. He has become her oncologist here in Los Angeles and he works closely with Dr. Jacob. The results of the scan were not great. There appeared to be several new tumors in the liver. Dr. Jacob and Dr. Vogl were consulted. They feel Farrah needs to come back to Germany immediately for another liver perfusion. "Immediately" means leaving here this coming Thursday, which is Thanksgiving Day, arriving in Frankfurt on Friday, and going straight to Dr. Vogl for the procedure. This was all quite a shock. I had to explain to Mimmo that I was leaving in three days to go back to

Germany. He was a little in shock, too, needless to say. He called Jimmy Van Patten, whom he had become friends with when the Van Pattens were at the clinic in September, and Jimmy said Mimmo could stay in his parents' guesthouse when I leave. I felt bad about leaving so soon, but we had no choice.

Farrah felt much worse than I did. She kept saying, "But Mimmo just got here. I don't want you to have to leave. I can see if I can get someone else to go."

"It's not an option," I replied firmly. "I'm going. I barely know him, for God's sakes!" Farrah acquiesced. "Okay, good. Besides, you have to film . . ." She can see right through me. She knows I would never let her go back to Germany without me, but also that I am relieved that I don't have to deal with this sexy Italian guy staying in my home.

### November 22, 2007 (Thanksgiving Day)

Farrah and I are sitting in first class on Lufthansa, wolfing down caviar and having a cocktail while I fill her in on the latest Mimmo details. It feels almost like we're going away on a pleasure trip, two girlfriends off to Europe on holiday! But the reality is that we're going back to Germany in hopes of saving her life. I don't know how she faces it with such an astonishing attitude. She doesn't complain. She doesn't feel sorry for herself or say, "Why did this happen to me?" She just gets on with it and asks them to bring more caviar. I think we're both kind of in denial about what the outcome could be. We just don't accept anything but that she'll be cured.

The last three days have been a blur. I hurriedly started making plans—plane reservations, ground transportation, the hotel in Frankfurt, and the time to see Dr. Vogl. I begged my part-time housekeeper to come and stay with the dogs while I was gone. But the hardest thing of all was telling my kids I wouldn't be cooking Thanksgiving dinner. Each of them asked me, "But, Mom, where will we eat Thanksgiving dinner? You always cook." I felt horribly guilty, but I had to go with Farrah, and I promised them I'd make up for it on Christmas. I really wanted them to understand that it wasn't about choosing my friend over them. It was about being there for someone who needed me more at this moment; it was a matter of life and death.

Before we left, I felt obligated to show Mimmo around L.A., at least a little, especially since I was ditching him. He really wanted to see the beach, so I drove him out to Malibu. We had a nice lunch at a lovely outdoor restaurant, took a walk on the pier, where he took pictures, and then we drove back. That night we went to my friend Nicollette Sheridan's birthday party, which her boyfriend, Michael Bolton, was throwing for her in a bowling alley in Hollywood. I wasn't sure how Mimmo was going to fit into the mix, especially not speaking a word of English, but he was just fine. In fact, all the attractive single women who were there were flirting with him. I hadn't been at all attracted to him until then, but after a Cosmopolitan, he started to look cuter. Still, when we got back to my house, I kissed him goodnight on the cheek and went to my bedroom.

Last night I had to pack to leave today, so he cooked a great Italian meal for us. After dinner, we sat by the fire, drank a

Ramazzotti, and chatted. My Italian was improving, that's for sure. Up until now, I'd been clearly sending him the signal that I wasn't interested in anything other than being platonic friends, and he had been very respectful of that. I told him as best as I could in Italian that I needed to get to know him better, that I didn't know anything about him or how many women he slept with, and that I was very cautious about getting physically involved with anyone, especially these days. God knows it's been forever since I've been in any kind of relationship. He said he had been with one woman for five years, that they had broken up almost a year ago, and that he hadn't really dated anyone since then. He said he was working all the time and didn't have the time to date. That was a relief. At least he wasn't some Italian playboy.

Then the mood gradually shifted. He kissed me softly and I let him, but with little response on my part. He kissed me again. I liked that he wasn't being pushy about it. And I liked the way he kissed me, so I let him kiss me more. I was definitely attracted to him. One thing led to another, and we ended up making love. It was very nice—a terrible word to describe lovemaking, I guess. But the earth didn't move, it was just warm and . . . nice. When it was time to go to bed, I said goodnight and went into my room and he went into his. I wasn't ready to sleep in the same bed with him; that would have been just too much too soon.

So now I'm on my way to Germany and he's staying in Los Angeles another week. I like him. I enjoyed his company, and I feel kind of attracted to him. But I don't know how I'll feel when I see him again. Right now, there are more important things to deal with.

### November 23, 2007

We arrived, dropped our bags off at the hotel, and went straight to Dr. Vogl's for Farrah's liver perfusion. It all went smoothly, and after a few hours in the recovery room, we returned to the hotel to spend the night. The driver who had picked us up at the airport told us there was a much better hotel than the "disco" hotel we had stayed at before. It was called the Villa Kennedy and it was very close to the hospital, so we decided to try it.

Impulsively we canceled our reservations at the disco hotel, which turned out to be a wise choice on our part. There was no comparison. We were so happy to be in a lovely room in a first-class hotel with great food. We got into our pajamas, ordered room service, ate, and settled down for the night.

### November 27, 2007

The past few days have been a blur of jet lag and IVs. We haven't even been outside the room. Farrah is feeling stronger and better.

### November 29, 2007

Mimmo returned from Los Angeles today. Tonight he took Farrah and me to dinner at a charming restaurant for a typical

Bavarian meal: duck, red cabbage, and potato dumplings. It was delicious. I translated his Italian into English for Farrah and vice versa. He looked more handsome than I'd remembered.

When we got back to the clinic, I was going to get out of the car with Farrah, but she looked at me and slyly said, "Why don't you two go have a drink and catch up?" (She knew *quite* well what she was doing.)

Mimmo seconded the idea, so he and I went to a small bar nearby and had several Ramazzotti's, my new favorite drink. He asked me if I wanted to come back to his house, which was a few blocks away. It's such a small town that everything is a few blocks away. I still wasn't sure how I really felt about him or if I was ready to resume where we had left off. Maybe it was better to just leave it at that and be friends. However, I think that Ramazzotti might have an aphrodisiacal effect on the brain, because I found myself back at his place. When we made love this time, for some reason, it was off the charts amazing! It was a fairly sleepless night since I don't sleep well in a new environment, and besides he was curled up to me way too closely, with his arm around me.

He drove me back to the clinic around 9 A.M. and as I tried to sneak quietly into my room, Farrah heard me. Now I was in for it.

"Well, the slut of Tegernsee is back!" Farrah called out from her adjoining room. She was already up with Dr. Jacob, gleefully awaiting my return and wanting "all the details." They both had quite a time at my expense. Farrah did greatly exaggerated imitations of me the rest of the trip—staggering into the room, disheveled and exhausted after my night of passion with the Italian chef. I think it gave her great pleasure that I was having this little romance here. She knows what I'm giving up to be with her in Germany, and she wants me to have a little happiness, a little fun, away from the clinic.

### ◈ December 1, 2007

Last night I had dinner with Mimmo at his restaurant. Farrah didn't feel up to coming, so he cooked some wonderful pasta and after we'd eaten we took it back to the clinic for her. She wanted to go to sleep early, so I went back to Mimmo's house. Again, it was absolutely wonderful. We made love all night. I never imagined I'd have this kind of hot sex again at this stage of my life. He told me that the reason he can make love to me like this is because he's in love with me. It sounds so romantic in Italian. "*Sono innamarato di te.*"

Tonight Farrah and I went with Dr. Jacob and her boyfriend, Manfred, to dinner at Mimmo's. Mimmo went all out to make a fabulous dinner for us. Ravioli with asparagus and Pecorino cheese and fresh fish with small roasted potatoes and spinach. He brought us a marvelous dessert called Crema Catalano, similar to flan but better. Farrah and I both think it's the best Italian food we've ever eaten. I went back to the clinic with Farrah afterward. I didn't want to leave her alone again for the night although she was feeling quite well. I, however, was exhausted.

I was lying in bed thinking about the past few days. It feels kind of strange and almost disloyal to be having this romantic love affair while I'm here with my best friend who is fighting cancer. It's probably just my overblown sense of guilt. Farrah doesn't see it that way at all. She's thrilled for me. She thinks I should go for it and that Mimmo is great for me. I like him a lot, but I'm pretty clear that it's just for now. Maybe God brought him into my life to help me get through all this. I sometimes don't take into account that it's very emotional and stressful for me because I'm so focused on Farrah. With what she's going through, I feel guilty thinking about myself.

## December 2, 2007

This morning Mimmo picked Farrah and me up and took us for a walk on a path along an incredibly beautiful lake about fifteen minutes away from the clinic. The day was like a gift from God; the sun was sparkling on the water, the mountains rising majestically in the background. Farrah was looking great and feeling better than she has in a long time. We walked for almost an hour, and although she was full of energy, I was exhausted and had to sit down and rest. She didn't let me hear the end of it, either! We had a wonderful time, laughing and joking. She felt so grateful for such a perfect day, and it made me happy to see her in such good spirits.

Farrah was tired from the day and wanted to talk to Ryan and go to bed early, so I went to dinner with Mimmo and some of his friends at a famous Bavarian beer garden. Many of the Germans were wearing their traditional Bavarian clothing: lederhosen for the men and dirndls for the women. It was like being in another era. I went back to Mimmo's afterward and ended up sleeping there. I guess I could hardly say I slept. It's a wonder I can even walk! He told me again that he's in love with me. I know he's hoping I'm going to tell him I'm in love with him, but the truth is that I can't honestly say that. I'm crazy about him and I'm sure attracted to him sexually, but I don't want to rush into anything. It's unusual for me to be this attracted to a man and not want it to be something more than it is. I know I'm not going to spend the rest of my life with Mimmo.

◈ *December 4, 2007*

We left for Frankfurt at 6:30 A.M. Well, actually 7:15 by the time Farrah got downstairs. Late again. It took us almost six hours to get there, with two big accidents stopping traffic for miles. Dr. Vogl performed another laser surgery, and again it was terribly painful for her because they didn't put her under. I could never do this. Afterward I told Farrah that I would have said to Dr. Vogl, "You either knock me out or I'm getting off this operating table and getting the hell outta here!"

She laughed because she knew I meant it. I don't know how she endures it with such resilience. Her will seems unbreakable; she just does what she has to do. They kept her overnight in the hospital again and I slept in the room with her.

◈ *December 5, 2007*

Farrah is still in a lot of pain today. Much more so than the last time. Dr. Vogl came into the room this morning to examine her. He said it was one of the largest tumors he had ever removed and that it was a very dangerous surgery because of where it was located, next to a major vessel. We'd had no idea that it would be so difficult, and quite frankly he hadn't, either, until he actually got into the surgery. They did some blood work, and her liver enzymes were dangerously high, so high that one of the other doctors said she could die if the number continued to rise.

I was in a panic. I called Dr. Jacob and she said to get Farrah back to the clinic so she could treat her. There was much conferring, and the doctors were adamant that she should stay another night, but in typical Farrah fashion, she insisted we leave. It was against my better judgment, but when Farrah makes up her mind, there's no stopping her. When the doctors left the room, she had me call the driver from the clinic, who was waiting downstairs, and tell him to come up. He helped her into a wheelchair while I grabbed all our belongings, and we fled like thieves in the night.

◈ *December 8, 2007*

We were supposed to leave tomorrow, but Dr. Jacob wants us to delay it until at least Monday. Farrah is still in no shape to travel. I had dinner with her in the room, and when she went to sleep, I met Mimmo for a drink. We went back to his house and made love, but I went back to the clinic to sleep so I could be there if Farrah needed me. I always tell her to wake me if she needs anything in the night, but she never does. Sometimes she'll tell me in the morning that she was up for hours in pain, and when I ask her why she didn't wake me, she always says, "I didn't want to bother you."

I tell her that if it were me, I'd damned sure bother her!

### December 9, 2007

More delays. After examining her, Dr. Jacob said we should put the flight off until Tuesday or Wednesday. I won't know until tomorrow morning if that's possible. Farrah started to feel a little better toward the end of the day, so she came to dinner with Dr. Jacob, Mimmo, and me. But before dinner was over, she was starting to have a lot of pain again. I went back to the clinic so that I could stay with Farrah. I figured that I'd be able to change the flight in the morning and I would see Mimmo tomorrow night.

### December 10, 2007

Farrah woke up early this morning feeling better and wanted to go. By the time they said we could change the flight, she was ready and the car was downstairs. It's the first time I've ever seen her be ready to leave early! When she's ready to go, she's really ready to go. I didn't think it was wise to travel against Dr. Jacob's advice, but there wasn't anything I could do to dissuade her at this point. I called Mimmo to say good-bye and he was really sad. I felt rather sad, too. I'd really thought we'd have one last night together.

We got to the airport and were met by the Lufthansa representative and escorted into the VIP lounge. Farrah went into the bathroom and was gone a long time. When I went in to see if she was all right, I found her doubled over and her face was ashen. She said the pain had started again.

"Are you sure we should go?" I asked, knowing full well what her answer would be. She assured me she would take her pain medication and she would be fine.

"Just get me on the plane and I'll make it," she said.

"You're a very stubborn young lady," I replied, half teasing, half serious.

The first part of the flight was fine. We ate and chatted and bought duty-free crap like blushers and nail polish. Then she fell asleep and I read for a while. After an hour or so, I went to the toilet and when I returned, she was lying there awake, crying softly.

"What's the matter, honey? I just looked over and saw you crying."

"It's the pain . . . ," she answered through her tears.

"Do you want me to get the shot ready?" I asked. Thank God I'd had the foresight to ask Dr. Jacob to give me a pain shot for her just in case she needed it. She nodded and I prepared the shot and she gave it to herself in the abdomen. The pain began to subside soon after, and just before she fell asleep, I said with a little smile, "I don't want to say I told you so, but I told you so!" She smiled back at me sheepishly, and we both laughed, my stubborn little friend and me.

This past month has been surreal: watching Farrah suffer through this agonizing experience and at the same time having this romantic affair with Mimmo. But Farrah is my priority, and any man who says he's in love with me will have to understand that. This is a whole new me! I remember the time in Aspen years ago when another friend of mine was sick with the flu and I had just met this man I was very attracted to. She said that she felt abandoned by me because I was spending so much time with him. Looking back, I'm sorry to say that she was right. In the past, I always put the man first, and everything else took a backseat—including my own needs. Now I realize that men come and go, but a friendship between two women needs to be nourished and cherished for the gift that it is.

I look over at Farrah and she's sleeping quietly and peacefully. There is no doubt in my mind that I have made the right decision.

### January 1, 2008

I can't believe we're actually in 2008. Life feels like it's moving too fast and there's not enough of it left. This experience with Farrah has made me realize how fleeting life can be, how it can change in a heartbeat and never be the same. It's so important to live in the moment and love in the moment and cherish the people you care about. I've never been particularly good about living in the moment, but after the last year, I'm determined to get better.

I just read the lesson for today in *A Course in Miracles,* one of my favorite spiritual teachings, the one that Marianne Williamson reintroduced. It's about not looking to the world to find answers. I really get that now. Nothing in the material world can make you safe; nothing can save you from life's challenges and trials—no man, no person, no situation, no amount of money—only a connection to a Higher Power or God, or whatever one chooses to call this power in the universe that's greater than we are. As much as I try, I'm not sure I totally understand it. I'm trying not to get frightened about the future, but I don't see the solution to my dwindling financial situation. I keep surrendering it to God, trusting there's an answer, but on the other hand, I don't want to just sit and do nothing and be paralyzed in fear. Yet I don't know what to do. The television show that seemed like a sure thing hasn't been given a go, and there doesn't appear to be any other work in my future. I see Tina making plans for building her new house and growing old in it, while I'm the same age and I don't have the resources to know I'm taken care of for the rest of my life. I can't even imagine where that kind of financial security could come from at this stage of the game. I'm sure I'm in the same boat as a lot of women my age. It's a scary place to be. I just have to trust that it will work out.

And now we're leaving again for Farrah's follow-up treatment. We're going to fly with Bren Simon on her plane to Germany and go straight to the clinic. So I have barely three weeks to try to catch up on things here and get ready for the next trip. My kids don't like me being gone so much. It's funny that they're young adults but they still come to me whenever they have a problem. I guess that's what mothers are for. And my dogs hate it when I leave. They start to mope around and give me long, baleful looks as soon as they see the suitcases come out. Guilt, guilt, guilt. I have problems in the house to deal with; most of all I have to decide if I'm going to try to sell it now or wait until my money runs out. I must say that sometimes it's a relief to go off to Germany and escape reality for a while. It's just that it's always waiting for me when I come back.

*Birthdays were always big for us. For as long as I can remember, Farrah's been at my birthdays and I've been at hers. It wasn't just tradition; it just didn't feel right without each other there. Oh sure, we missed some here and there, but by and large, if it was possible, we were together. Whether at her house or mine, a restaurant, or a party somewhere, we almost always celebrated getting older and wiser together.*

*For her birthday in February 2008, where this photo was taken, we all crowded into Mimmo's, across the street from the clinic. He made her a fabulous birthday dinner. The first course, which Farrah loved, was thinly sliced beets, Pecorino cheese, and arugula. The second course was taglioni pasta with a hint of butter and truffles—our favorite pasta there. The next course was fish, a lovely sea bass. Then came the birthday cake and champagne. Farrah enjoyed every bite. We drank, we ate, then they played Stevie Wonder's "Happy Birthday to You" and we danced.*

*Farrah was in great spirits. My ex George was there with Dr. Barbara, as were my son Sean and his girlfriend Caleigh, our friend Lili Zanuck, Dr. Jacob, and Anna Danenza. Dr. Jacob even wore a dirndl, a traditional Bavarian dress.*

*Finally, as the evening was winding down, Farrah got up to make some toasts. First, she turned to Dr. Jacob.*

*"Thank you for saving my life," she said, and Dr. Jacob nodded back.*

*And then, flashing a big smile, she raised her glass to me.*

*"To my best friend. It wouldn't have been possible without you."*

# GOOD NEWS . . . BAD NEWS

❖ *February 10, 2008*

Finally! A good-news trip! We've been gone from L.A. for over three weeks now. I haven't written this entire trip and I don't know where to start. I haven't had a free minute, it seems.

When Farrah and I arrived at the clinic, our driver pointed out that two paparazzi had followed us and were taking pictures from their car. I ran to film them and they took off. Now they knew we were here, so we'd have to keep a constant watch for them every time we went out.

Sean, his girlfriend Caleigh, and his friend Elijah, Cher's son, are also here, as well as George and Barbara and our friend Lili Zanuck. It's like one big party.

The day after we arrived, Farrah and I had to go to Frankfurt so she could have one more laser surgery with Dr. Vogl. "I feel like a dog being taken to the vet," she said en route to the surgery. "A dog always starts to shake when it nears the destination because it remembers the last visit." And yet she pushes through the fear and the trepidation because she wants to live. Such courage.

This surgery was not as difficult as the last one, although the procedure was just as painful. We spent the night in the hospital, and the next morning I accompanied her as they wheeled her to the MRI. Afterward we went into Dr. Vogl's office, Farrah still in her hospital gown and in considerable pain. "Dr. In and Out" sat with us for an unusually long time.

"The last laser surgery in December was really dangerous," he said. "It was difficult to decide what to do. You could have died from it." We sat there in stunned silence.

Then he went on to say that he was able to get the rest of the tumors today and that the remaining ones were already necrotic (meaning they're dying or dead). "So you are now tumor free," he said matter-of-factly.

I wanted to be perfectly clear: "You mean she doesn't have any more tumors?" I asked incredulously.

"She has no more active tumors." Then he quickly added, "In the liver."

Farrah and I hugged each other in celebration; this was the greatest news we'd had in a long time. We supposed afterward that he only wanted to go on record in the area he was certain about. But nevertheless, we were over the moon.

When we arrived back at the clinic, Dr. Jacob met us and explained that, while Farrah has no active tumors in her body, she still has cancer cells in her blood, and that's where the other treatments come in: the special antibodies and anticancer drugs, even some plant derivatives that are known to kill cancer cells. The war is far from over, but a major battle has just been won.

We all celebrated Farrah's birthday at Mimmo's restaurant at a little birthday party I organized for her. It was a true celebration, and she was elated. "This is the best birthday I've ever had," she announced, "because I'm alive." It was an incredibly meaningful and special evening.

It sounds crazy that someone would be thankful for being sick—but that's what Farrah said to Dr. Jacob earlier today. "I'm grateful that I got cancer . . . because now I see that I can make a difference." I wasn't surprised that she said this. She's been so moved by how many people have reached out to her, not just with get-well wishes, but with questions, requests for information, and gratitude. For the last year and a half that this has been going on, I've never seen Farrah once question the fact that this was happening to her or feel sorry for herself. She just accepts this for what it is and pushes forward; she deals with whatever is on her plate very methodically and doesn't waste time wallowing in self-pity. But this brutal disease has to have happened for a reason. There had to be some purpose God had in mind for Farrah Fawcett. She's been thinking about that a lot these days, especially now that her cancer is technically "in remission." She has a new lease on life, and she's realizing how much she could help others who are also battling a life-threatening illness. She could open people's eyes to other forms of cancer treatments that aren't yet available in the United States. She could start a foundation for research and use it to help people who can't afford to try other methods. She's even started to think that what we've been filming all these months could be an impactful documentary. The possibilities are endless. And for this, she is grateful. It has given her life a new mission, a new definition.

During this whole trip, I'd been filming, not only for us, but also for a piece on Farrah to be aired on *Entertainment Tonight*.

During the last trip to Germany, I came up with the idea to do our own footage, so that we could show how great Farrah was looking and feeling. I wanted to put a stop to all the horrible tabloid articles saying she was dying. Take that! She was angry and fed up with being stalked all the time by the paparazzi. They would try to get the worst possible shot of her and then sell it to the tabloids or get video footage of her coming out of her doctor's office and sell it to the entertainment programs for big bucks. The *National Enquirer* came out with one headline that blared on the front page: "Farrah Given Weeks to Live!" The article said the cancer had spread to her pancreas and she was dying. It was completely unfounded. There wasn't a word of truth to it and she was furious.

So we decided to fight fire with fire. *ET* aired our footage of Farrah looking radiant and energetic, walking by the lake, celebrating at her birthday party, and even having a snowball fight on a snow-covered mountain. Would a dying woman be having a snowball fight? Farrah, always competitive, pounded me with snowballs, one after the other. She was full of strength and verve. Of course, she had an unfair advantage—I was trying to film! Finally, in self-defense, I handed the camera to Mimmo, who had driven us. I got a few good shots in myself, but she was clearly the winner . . . in more ways than one. We felt that maybe this would shut the rags up for a while, and it succeeded, at least momentarily. Another win for our side!

Mimmo and I are still going hot and heavy. I really like him, and he's very sweet to me and to my son. Sean adores him, and loves his food. He, Caleigh, and Cher's son, Elijah, go over to his restaurant every day for lunch, and Mimmo cooks them Sean's favorite pasta: baked penne with prosciutto, tomato sauce, and mozzarella. Sometimes I join them. Mimmo keeps telling me he's in love with me, and finally one night, in the heat of passion, I said (faintly), "Me, too." I'm not even sure he heard me, and it's just as well because I'm just not sure if I'm really in love with him. It's great for now, but the bottom line is, I know it's not forever.

All in all, it's been a positive trip—but I'm exhausted and emotionally drained. Right now I feel like I want to cry and have someone take care of me—like a little girl that wants to curl up in her parents' arms and have them tell her everything will be okay. I feel like I always have to be the strong one and take care of everyone else—it's overwhelming sometimes. It's been that way all my life. I had to grow up too fast, too soon, and take care of my mother, who was a prescription drug addict and suffered from depression and ill health. Then it was husbands and children. I guess everyone dealing with a loved one who has a serious illness feels this way from time to time. It's human. It's impossible not to.

And yet I feel guilty even thinking about myself, or complaining, when Farrah is fighting for her life. I'm not the one battling cancer. Ever since this started I've been working to let go of my fears and get out of my head—get outside of myself. During the moments when everything feels like it's piling up, I've been trying to remember the words of Rabbi Eitan that I heard all those months ago, around the time that Farrah was first diagnosed. I need to be thankful, get past myself, and do things for others.

He's right. There's no two ways about it. This experience has been truly life-changing for both Farrah and me. A year ago I would have been a wreck, but now what I really feel is gratitude. There is so much to be grateful for now. Farrah has no active tumors and her future is looking very optimistic, my children are all okay for the moment, and I have to surrender the future to God. What I'm doing to help my friend is the most important thing I could do right now, and I have to trust that everything else will be taken care of.

### April 20, 2008

Mimmo is arriving in Los Angeles tonight. I'm really nervous. I don't know how I'll feel with him being in my house for over a week. Will I feel crowded? Eight days is a long time in close quarters, and it sure brings up my fear of intimacy and feeling claustrophobic. What if I'm not as attracted to him here on my home turf? I guess I just have to be open and not be judgmental or worried about what my friends will think about him. That's the superficial part of me, and that's not who I want to be. Also, I don't need to try to make this fit into a certain mold. Even though it's probably not forever, I can enjoy it for now.

### April 23, 2008

I went with Farrah and Ryan today to get her scans. I felt sure it was going to be okay, or at least I didn't allow myself to think otherwise. She seemed really calm, but I'm sure she was nervous. Who wouldn't be? This would be the first scan since she was pronounced tumor free in February. Ryan was the worried one. It was almost as if he expected bad news.

Afterward Dr. Piro explained that one of the old tumors appeared to be active again, and two other tiny new ones had also shown up on the scan. On top of that, there appeared to be some activity in the rectal area, where the original cancer had started. He took us into a room where the technicians showed us the scans. It was kind of surreal. We were all in this dark room, watching these screens of her body while they pointed out the various places they thought were possibly active tumors. She started to cry softly. I was filming it all, although it was so dark you could only see the screens and the outline of everyone in there.

The last trip to Germany had been so positive; we were so jubilant; but now our mood had shifted drastically. While we always worry whenever there's a new scan, I don't think any of us had expected this news. Ryan pulled her close and said, "It's okay. We'll beat this." Farrah pulled herself together, and before leaving the room even turned to thank the doctors who had given her the bad news. She and Ryan went outside into the hallway and he held her while she nestled her head on his shoulder. You could see the pain and fear in his eyes, but he was being brave for her.

We went downstairs, got into our cars, and left. Farrah and Ryan went back to her place to try to find the last scan from Dr. Vogl. All the scans they did today will have to be sent to him in Germany for the ultimate interpretation, since what appeared active could be the old dying tumors or inflammation. I pray that's all it is, but I have a sinking feeling in the pit of my stomach.

### April 26, 2008

I haven't had any time to write with Mimmo here. He came for an eight-day visit this time. I was really nervous that eight days would be too long—maybe just a little too much togetherness. Would I be able to handle it? Actually, I'll miss him when he leaves, but I think I'll also be a little relieved to get back to normal. God knows I need to recuperate from having so much sex! Also, I find myself keeping him at a distance. He continues to tell me he's in love with me, but I'm not "in love," whatever that means anyway. I'm just trying to stay in the moment and not analyze it too much, but most of all not judge. He's not the stable, mature man I'd like if it were to be permanent. But this is who God has put in front of me in this moment. He's sweet, intelligent, sexy, handsome, and hardworking. And he's very good to me. He cooks great food for me; he washed all my windows; he's great to my kids and my dogs. It's kind of like having a wife, in a way. And on top of it he makes me feel safe and protected, strangely enough.

Farrah's scans still haven't reached Dr. Vogl. It's ridiculous that she should have to wait until Monday to know what's going on. I know she's anxious and scared. She was starting to feel well and exercise a little. We have been going to Pilates together and she was starting to get stronger. In fact, it annoys me no end that she's way stronger than me on the machines. Her attitude is "Look at me! Even with cancer I can kick your butt!"

### April 30, 2008

So much is happening—too fast. It feels like life is spinning by so quickly I can't catch my breath. Farrah's results came back from Germany, and she *does* have two or three new tumors in her liver. The primary one, the original site, shows some activity and needs to be biopsied.

We have to go back to Germany within the next two weeks. Of course, I'll go with her. Having said that, I feel a little depressed about leaving my home and my dogs again so soon. I can't seem to get caught up. And I'll be missing my birthday. Am I avoiding reality by continuing to go to Germany? My heart tells me I have to be with my friend, no matter what, and just trust that God will take care of me.

Mimmo left Monday night. I was sad to see him go but relieved in a way. On the one hand, he's taking my mind off how things are with Farrah; on the other, I feel like I can't get anything done when he's here. I'm just confused as to how I feel about him. Very confused. He's very hardheaded and states his opinion as though it's absolute fact—silly things like which car is better than another—and yet I find myself disputing it. I guess I'm pretty stubborn, too. I do the same thing with George. He and Mimmo are similar in that respect. It must be the Leo in them. But why do I feel the need to challenge them and to be right? Why can't I just enjoy

Mimmo for the fun of it, like Farrah suggests? Again, it's a way of deflecting closeness, pushing him away like I did with that little boy who brought me flowers when I was three. I shoved him down and he hit his head on the pavement. Poor little guy. He's probably still on some therapist's couch somewhere.

I just spoke to Marianne. How serendipitous that she would call at this instant. She said what I'm doing with Farrah is a holy thing, that being a friend and going with her is the highest form of love. And that I have a great guy there who loves me. God will take care of the rest. Be in the moment. She said the future is in your head and so is the past. It's about being in the present moment and placing the future in the hands of God.

## May 2, 2008

Good news, finally! Sean's case was dismissed. I've never felt so relieved. Over the last couple of days, I've been sick with this virus from hell, so maybe now I won't feel as stressed and I'll get healthy. Tonight I went to a dinner at Lili and Dick Zanuck's house for Dr. Jacob, who was in L.A. to see Farrah and some other patients. I've introduced her to all these people who now just love her: Lili, Cher, Farrah, Carole Bayer Sager, and a few of my other friends and acquaintances as well. Dr. Jacob is so busy with patients, I'm lucky if I can get her attention these days. She thinks a lot of my problems are in my mind. God knows maybe they are, but they sure seem real enough to me!

The dinner was really lovely, although four members of the

Germany group didn't show up because they got lost. George and Barbara were there. I still have some mixed feelings about that. It's nothing against Barbara; I really like her. It's just that I have some strange sense of abandonment now that George is actually in a relationship with someone. I always wondered how I would feel if it ever happened, but somehow I didn't think it would. I think, in some weird way, our connection has kept me from being fully open to being with another man. I've always felt such loyalty toward George. I guess it's like a brother or a father, but it's even more than that. I've always felt like we're soul mates, and I feel a little thrown by the whole thing with Barbara happening out of the blue

Complicating all this was the fact that Mimmo is still in the picture. I'm still confused about that, too. I want to be open to being with him, but although I'm ashamed to admit it, I feel like I want more. More what? More stability, more security, more of a feeling of safety? Is that so terrible of me or just totally honest? Am I being superficial or just clear about the kind of life I want to live at this point? Marianne says I can have the "more" on my own; I can create my own security. But how in the world could that happen? I guess anything is possible. Miracles can happen, right?

❧ *May 18, 2008*

My birthday. Because it turned out that we're not leaving for Germany until later in the month, I was able to enjoy having my birthday in L.A. I stayed home all day, ostensibly to relax and enjoy myself. Ha! Instead I felt horribly anxious (I always do on my birthday). I worried about everyone having a good time at my party. Farrah wasn't able to come. Ryan drove in from the beach to pick her up, but she was sick from having three consecutive days of scans. She called me while she was trying to get ready, but I could hear how weak she was.

"Don't try to come, honey. I'll miss you terribly, but I don't want you to feel pressured to show up somewhere."

The party was lovely and everyone had a great time. I decided to have my favorite lychee martini and eat everything I wanted, including the chocolate marble birthday cake, and hang the consequences. Carole and Bob Daly had organized everything beautifully in the upstairs room at Mr Chow, my favorite restaurant. Twenty of my friends were there, including Jaclyn Smith, Nicollette Sheridan, Raquel Welch, Tina, George, and my son Sean.

I feel so grateful to have such wonderfully generous friends, especially Carole and Bob. I got some really beautiful presents, including a Chanel bag from George and a beautiful Balenciaga pearl necklace from Carole and Bob, but certainly the most unusual present was from Tina Sinatra: an orphaned baby elephant in Africa. She made me his sponsor. Has she lost her mind? I have three kids that cause me enough stress—I sure don't need a baby elephant. I mean, of all the things I could use! I asked her if I could make a purse out of it when it's bigger (it was a joke, I swear). After she showed me his picture, I fell in love: his name is Shimba, and he still drinks milk from a bottle. I've decided I want to go visit him in Africa one day.

When I was driving home, I was smiling to myself, recalling

all the laughs we had this evening. Then I remembered there was something blatantly missing: Farrah. She would have loved the food and the company and laughed at my crack about the elephant purse. It was a wonderful celebration . . . but it feels a little strange, a little hollow, without my sweet friend.

◈ *May 20, 2008*

Farrah called this morning and I barely recognized her voice, it was so weak. She'd been up since six o'clock throwing up and in terrible pain. I called Dr. Piro to see if he could go to her house, but he wanted her to come to his clinic so he could do tests. Ryan bundled her up and took her there, and I hurriedly got ready to go meet them.

When I arrived, she was still throwing up nonstop. The medications they were giving her for the pain and nausea weren't working yet. This was like a replay of the time in the Frankfurt clinic that she got so sick after the liver chemo perfusion and threw up seventy-five times.

God, it's so hard to see her go through this agony. I almost have to detach from my body and go somewhere else in my mind, it's so painful. That's what I've always done. When my son Ash was in the emergency room with his fractured skull, I was there, but none of it seemed real. It's the same with Farrah. I walk through it all, but often I feel like I've disassociated myself from the reality of it.

By around five o'clock, when the vomiting still hadn't stopped,

Farrah was still adamantly refusing to go to the hospital. She hates hospitals, plain and simple. It's why we're always rushing to get home from Germany: she can't bear to spend one more minute in the hospital or clinic if she doesn't have to. Something had to be done, though. Neither Dr. Piro or I was getting anywhere, and she needed medical attention. Finally, I called Ryan and said, "You have to convince Farrah that she has to go into the hospital. We're having no luck." I knew he'd get her to change her mind. He has a way with her; she trusts him and respects his opinions. So she stopped protesting and listened to him, and we were finally able to take her next door to St. John's in a wheelchair, wrapped up in a blanket. Finally, the vomiting stopped. But we're obviously not leaving for Germany tomorrow.

nook

What if you could
hold Barnes & Noble
in your hand and carry
it with you everywhere
you go?
Now you can.
With just one simple tap
on a color touchscreen
you can wirelessly
download your favorite
books, newspapers and
magazines within seconds.
Introducing nook.
By Barnes & Noble.

BARNES & NOBLE

*Nothing like a change of scenery.*

*After our fourth trip to Germany, when they declared Farrah tumor free, we went to Mexico with our friend Bren Simon. It was March 2008, and this was our spring break. We flew down on Bren's G5 and stayed at this incredibly beautiful house in Punta Mita. Farrah and I would lie in the sun, and there was a huge staff that would wait on us hand and foot. We ate every five minutes: they'd bring us watermelon juice, guacamole and chips, quesadillas, and margaritas at night.*

*There was this ATV, and I was determined to learn how to drive the thing. So I took one spin around by myself, then I pulled up alongside Farrah.*

*"Hop on!" I yelled.*

*She gave me a look like I was completely insane (which I probably was), crossed herself, and got on. At first it was kind of jerky, and I was going no faster than two miles an hour. Then I got the hang of it and we flew through the sand, laughing all the way. We went driving back and forth, up and down the beach. We drove past a wedding, and a guy came out and yelled at us for making too much noise. We sped away laughing.*

*We were there for a week, and it was a slice of heaven—the last time I remember Farrah really feeling good for a prolonged period of time. We talked so many times about going back there, but we never made it.*

# CANCER FOR A DAY

———◆———

I woke up with horrible anxiety this morning. An elephant-sitting-on-my-chest kind of anxiety. I'm worried about Farrah, the looming trip to Germany, and, of course, as always, my future.

Farrah called from the hospital. She'd slept through the night, the MRI was okay, and the doctor said she could go home and rest there. She said they were giving her Dilaudid for the pain. I resisted the impulse to ask if I could have some. I've never had it, but according to drug addicts, it's like heroin. Sounds mighty attractive right now. Maybe I can become a drug addict since I can't tolerate enough liquor to become an alcoholic.

On top of everything else, I had a Pap smear done two weeks ago and it came back irregular. I freaked out and spoke to the gynecologist, who said this sometimes happens but the subsequent test they run would probably come back normal. I asked what happened if it didn't, and she said they do something called a colposcopy, which magnifies the cells of the cervix to see if there are any irregularities. If there are, then they have to do a biopsy to see if it's cancer. She said not to worry, because there was only a 5 percent chance it would be positive. I'd feel better if it was, like, 1 percent.

Of course, I'm already thinking it's cancer. I don't even know if it's positive yet. But after all I've seen Farrah going through, cancer terrifies me. And I've also seen how it operates: it can come out of nowhere, when you least expect it, when you're totally not prepared. It doesn't play fair.

I called my old gynecologist, and she said my last Pap smear in December was fine and that other things can affect a Pap smear. She said I shouldn't be concerned, so I decided—for now—to put it out of my mind. I don't need one more thing to worry about.

### *May 25, 2008*

Farrah and I were supposed to leave for Germany tomorrow, but I was at her house last night and she seemed too weak to travel. This morning I changed everything to Wednesday. It's a big relief to her and to me. I can't think straight. I still haven't packed. I have piles of clothes on my bed and it's too confusing to figure out what to take. I look like I'm going on a tour of Europe instead of to a medical clinic in Germany.

### *May 28, 2008*

Finally, Farrah and I got off to Frankfurt. Well, barely. I arrived at her house at 2:00 for a 4:25 P.M. departure. We were supposed to be at the airport by 2:45 at the latest. It looked like a bomb had struck: suitcases still open and half packed, clothes everywhere. She was wandering around, putting a few things here and a few things there.

I was determined not to get angry or stressed. Just detach and let it go. If we miss the plane, we'll get another one, I suppose— we'll just have a lot of pissed-off doctors on the other end. Not to mention the travel agent, who's changed this reservation about ten times now. It's Farrah's surgery, and if she misses it, it's her problem. Those rationalizations all sounded good, and I actually meant them until about 2:45 when we still weren't anywhere near leaving. Also, it was a Wednesday, and my astrologer had said, "Under no circumstances can you fly on Thursday."

By 3:00, I had started to panic a little, but I was determined not to show it. The last time we went, the exact same thing happened. I didn't speak to Farrah all the way to the airport I was so pissed. I decided to go downstairs and wait in the car, where I could do some deep breathing.

I don't know why it's always like this. No matter how many days in advance she has to pack, Farrah still ends up late, with everything all over the place. Everyone is in a panic but her. It's as if she has no concept of time. She finally arrived downstairs, perfectly cool. I don't know how. No one else was. I'd spoken to the airport greeter three times, and he kept telling me that if we got there later than 3:15 our luggage might not make it on the plane. Okay, that's a deal blower for me. If my luggage doesn't go, neither do I!

Long story short, we made it in the nick of time, with Benny, her houseman, driving like he was in the Indy 500. Farrah was calm and chatty.

"Well, once I'm in the car," she said, "it's out of my control. And besides, they always wait."

"Well, missy, one day they won't!" I retorted snippily, while quietly praying that, as much as I'd like to teach her a lesson, it wouldn't be today.

The Lufthansa people were waiting for us, of course, and we breezed through, except for the annoying paparazzi, who followed us all the way to the gate. I was filming them filming her. It was quite a commotion. I was surprised the airport police didn't arrest the whole lot of them.

The flight was really pleasant. We ate mounds of caviar on the plane, which more than made up for the leathery chicken and mediocre dessert. Farrah fell asleep, as she always does in anything that moves, and slept the entire trip. I took an Ativan and slept for four hours, which for me is a record.

◈ *May 29, 2008*

We arrived in Frankfurt this morning, dropped our bags off at the Villa Kennedy, and went straight to see Dr. Vogl. He did an MRI and then talked with us.

"There are four new tumors," he said with a blank expression. "I will do the perfusion in the morning."

We went back to the hotel, had relaxing "anti–jet lag" massages, and then got ready to go downstairs and meet Dr. Vogl and his wife in the bar for a drink. I went downstairs first, since Farrah was, not surprisingly, running late. I have to cut her some slack on the lateness, she's been going through such a difficult time. Dr. Vogl was alone, and he and I had a chance to talk. I asked him how he felt it was going.

"You're her best friend, right?" he asked.

"Yes," I said. I could sense something was coming.

"I'm concerned by what I saw on the scan. She has more than four new tumors, but I don't want her to know. She will lose hope."

I was shocked. He hadn't been completely truthful with her. "So what will you do?" I asked.

"Continue the perfusions, but more often," he said. "I'm concerned there's a seedbed somewhere else and they're coming from there."

"Has the original site been checked lately?" I asked.

"I'm going to do that tomorrow," he answered.

"So what does this mean? If you had to estimate, how long do you think she has?" I held my breath as I waited for his answer.

He thought. "Maybe three years . . . maybe five."

"But can't Dr. Jacob come up with something that will kill the seed ones, the ones in her blood?" I asked.

"It's possible," he answered. "This is what she must try to do."

I was afraid of the answer but had to ask: "Do people ever get completely cured of this?"

He pursed his lips and shook his head. Shook his head no. Again, he cautioned, "You must not tell her. She has a strong will. That's very important."

So what do I do now? Suddenly I have this knowledge and I don't dare share it with anyone. Is that the right thing to do? I sure wouldn't want Farrah to know and give up hope. But do I have the right to keep this to myself? I feel like I'm harboring a horrible secret. I wish Dr. Vogl hadn't told me.

## May 30, 2008

Farrah's liver perfusion went well today. Now she's in the recovery room and in quite a lot of pain. We wanted to spend the night at the hotel, but Dr. Jacob insisted she come back to the clinic so she can treat her. It's now 7 P.M. and I've come back to the hotel to get our luggage. Farrah is still in the makeshift recovery room in the hospital, which is really a supply room. The real recovery rooms are filled with other people. Maybe this is just the way they do it in Germany, but the people here are treated like cattle. They wheel them on the stretchers into a large hallway and just leave them lined up to wait for surgery. It's ridiculous to leave someone like Farrah lying on a stretcher in plain view of anyone who might have a camera. They're certainly not set up for VIP treatment.

I had a chance to speak to Dr. Vogl again. He said it went very well and he feels much more positive than he did yesterday. I brightened. "So tell me again, how long do you feel she may have?" I asked.

"Oh, she's in good shape," he said. "She can live quite a while."

"You mean like three to five years?" I asked, hoping for more. He looked pensive.

"That's long," he said. I didn't try to question him further. I guess I didn't want to know anymore.

Farrah got quite sick from the chemo, so Dr. Vogl decided to travel in the car with us. He had to go visit his ailing mother near Munich, and it was on our way (or so he said). In any case, he'd be in the car with us in case she got worse. The driver made a bed for her in the backseat of the van where she was able to sleep most of the way. I wasn't so fortunate. The two middle seats, where Dr. Vogl and I sat, were incredibly uncomfortable. I was so tired and so jet-lagged, I would have killed to lie down, but there was no place to put my head. Even so, I kept falling asleep and waking up with my head falling over in some weird, cramped position.

The trip seemed endless. We stopped at some awful roadside café to eat something, and Farrah woke up and gamely came with us. She wanted to order a Whataburger, but Dr. Vogl insisted on soup. It looked like the dishwater. I know she would have eaten a huge greasy hamburger if he hadn't been there.

Then we got back in the van only to find out that, after having already driven several hours, we were still three hours away from the place Dr. Vogl was going, which really wasn't directly on our way after all. When we had dropped him off, we were still two hours away from the clinic. Truly the trip from hell! We finally arrived there at 2 A.M. We checked into our rooms but were wide awake, so we talked until 5 A.M. I finally took an Ativan and went to sleep. I woke up and looked at my watch, which I thought read 8:30. I'd only slept three and a half hours, so I took another Ativan. Then I looked closer at my watch and saw that it was actually 2:30

in the afternoon. I couldn't believe I'd been so stupid, but then the Ativan started to kick in and I couldn't stay awake even though I wanted to. I fell back into a drugged sleep until 6:30 P.M.

P.S. I've been calling UCLA every day to see if my test has come back. Finally, I called one more time. I got the nurse on the phone and she looked it up on the computer and the Pap smear was still abnormal. I almost fell through the floor. Now I was freaked. I paged the doctor and finally got through to her. She reassured me that it wasn't that big of a deal and that there was no immediate rush. We could wait until I get back for the next step, which is the colposcopy, but it might make more sense just to have it done here. I'm going to talk to Dr. Jacob about it and possibly see a doctor in Munich, Dr. Rotorooter. I call him that because I can't remember his real name. Anyway, it's close enough.

## June 1, 2008

Mimmo called last night. He asked if I wanted to have dinner, so we went to this place up in the mountains with a magnificent view of the lake and the surrounding villages. Then we went back to his house and spent the night making love. I really enjoy being with him. I hate to be so superficial, but part of it is that he's so handsome, so chiseled, like a Roman statue. That and his phenomenal body. God, I sound like one of those old guys that are always with young women because they've got tight asses and big boobs. But he's very smart, has a good sense of humor, and is sweet as well. He adores me and always tries to please me. What could be bad about this? I know it's not forever, but it's nice for now.

Still, I'm shattered today. I never sleep well at his house. It's too bright and I forgot my sleep mask. And I can hear cars on the road outside. Then his damn alarm went off at seven thirty by accident. I had him drive me back to the clinic in hopes I could sleep a little more, but no such luck. Dr. Jacob came in, and I talked to her privately about my conversation with Dr. Vogl.

She pointed out that Farrah had made it through this year, which was a great accomplishment considering how ill she'd been when she first came to Germany, and she said she had some new ideas she wanted to go over with us. We went to Farrah's room, and Dr. Jacob went over her new plan.

"I want to change from herbatox to thalidomide," she explained. "This will stop the growth of cancerous cells."

She also wanted to use another form of stem cells that the Israelis are experimenting with; they supposedly go right to the cancer cells, like a torpedo aiming at a target, and kill them. She's brilliant and always on top of the latest cutting-edge treatments.

Farrah's feeling positive about the game plan. She has this incredible ability: she doesn't see anything as serious as it is until *after* the fact. When Dr. Vogl told her that she could easily have died from the laser surgery a few months ago (he'd never lasered such a large tumor before), or that no one looking at her X-rays a year ago would believe she's alive today, she was shocked. I felt the same way. We knew things were bad, but we had no idea they were *that* bad. Or maybe we just blocked out those thoughts from our minds? That's how we've approached this disease all along. One step at a time, do what you have to do, don't allow yourself to actually wonder "What if . . ." Dr. Vogl calls Farrah his "living experiment," and Dr. Jacob says Farrah is her "little miracle." Please, God, let it be so.

I'm not sure I could have gone through what Farrah has, and I'm sure that's why a lot of people give up. But her will, the same one that can make her controlling and a perfectionist, also pulls her through. As weak and sick and frail as she can seem at times, she's still Farrah with the fighting spirit, the sense of humor—the no-nonsense, no-BS Texas spitfire.

Farrah has never been one to back down from a confrontation. I remember one time when she was performing in *Extremities* on Broadway, and she and her assistant hopped into one of those New York City gypsy cabs. They weren't going far, just from the hotel to the theater, and when she got there the cabdriver pulled over to the curb.

"Gimme fifty bucks," he demanded.

Farrah looked him straight in the eye and said, "Absolutely not."

The driver, who didn't really care for her answer, pulled a knife on her. Her assistant begged her to hand over the money.

Never one to sit idly by and play the victim, Farrah responded in kind. Without hesitation, she took off her high-heeled shoe and threatened him right back with it. Then she grabbed twenty dollars out of her purse, threw it at him, and jumped out the door. Typical Farrah.

◈ *June 2, 2008*

I decided to go ahead and have the colposcopy here. The procedure is scheduled for tomorrow in Munich with Dr. Rotorooter, and I'm getting a little nervous. Dr. Jacob insisted I not wait till I get back to L.A. She feels it's more serious than my doctor at UCLA does. Dr. Rotorooter wants to biopsy and laser my cervix to prevent me from getting cervical cancer. He said it would take four weeks to heal—no baths, no hot tubs, and no sex! Well, it just seems a little radical. Farrah insisted on coming with me, but I said she should see how she feels. Boy, it just doesn't end. I'd like a little down time without a crisis, thank you.

◈ *June 3, 2008*

Farrah went with me to Dr. Rotorooter in Munich. Now I'm the patient, and she's the support system. Crazy how the tables have turned. As concerned as I am about her not being strong enough to make this trip, I'm so glad she came. I would be really terrified if I had to face this alone. And she would never let me.

The clinic was unlike any I've seen in the States. It's actually quite impressive—very modern, lovely art on the walls, a small dining area, a trolley with tea and cookies. It sure put UCLA to shame with its crowded waiting room, busy nurses whose attention you can never get, and tiny examination cubicles. The girls who worked at the Munich clinic were all dressed in white jeans.

"Look at that one," Farrah whispered mischievously. "She's got on black panties underneath . . ." We giggled. A gyno office staffed with sexpots!

They took us down a hallway and into one of the large private rooms where you get undressed and prepared for surgery and where you return for the recovery period. All very lovely. They brought in a beautiful vase of fresh flowers. I was mentally ticking off all the costs (probably another grand for the room and the flowers).

Then Dr. Rotorooter came in (his real name is Dr. Phutzen-reuter, but since he's a doctor of female plumbing, Rotorooter seemed apropos). He reminds me of a cross between Gene Wilder and Peter Sellers. Not sure if that's a good likeness for a doctor to have. I told him I didn't want to do the more radical surgery, just the biopsy, and then I'd come back later if I needed the more comprehensive one. I figured the biopsy would be fine. Only 5 percent chance of anything being wrong, according to the doctors in L.A. He really pressed for the complete procedure, but I insisted, so he relented.

Then the anesthesiologist, a tall, dapper, balding man, came in and introduced himself: Dr. Peter Wagner, "like the composer," he informed us. He immediately turned to Farrah and asked her if she'd ever known Steve McQueen, who was his favorite actor.

"No, sorry," she replied.

I figured I might as well score points with my anesthesiologist, so I piped up. "Hello? I knew him."

"Really?" he asked, lighting up and turning all his attention to me.

"Yes," I replied. "In fact, I dated him for a while in the seventies." That *really* impressed him. In fact, I think it even impressed Farrah, who hadn't known it before. I was never one to kiss and tell. Until now. It's funny that you can be such good friends with someone and still not know *everything* about them.

I've never seen anyone so interested in someone who's been dead so long; the doctor peppered me with questions about him. I finally had to fess up that I hadn't dated him for that long, and try to get him back to the subject at hand: sleep-inducing drugs. I said I didn't want to be put out for long and asked if he could give me Versed and Demerol, the combo they give you in the States when you have a colonoscopy. After the first time I had it, I understood why people do drugs. It was the most incredible sense of well-being and joy I've ever experienced.

Unfortunately, he didn't have them, so I had to settle for the one they use, which served its purpose but without the euphoria.

As the drugs were starting to take effect, a funny thing happened that Farrah took great glee in recounting later on. The nurse came in to put the green paper surgical cap on my head.

"Oh, don't put that thing on me," I protested. "My hair looks so beautiful." And then, according to Farrah (this part I don't remember), just as I was fading out, I looked at the doctor and said, "Wow, this feels great. Let's party!" That cracked her up.

I was only out a short time, and when I woke up, I was back in my room with Farrah. When the doctor finally came in, he said it all went well and that the results of the biopsy should be back in a day or so.

As I was preparing to leave, I went to the front desk, and the bill they gave me was for twenty-five hundred Euros, or about four thousand dollars. That seemed a little high to me for a biopsy, so as uncomfortable as it is for me to question a doctor about money, I summoned up the courage to ask him about it. He explained that it was for the anesthesiologist, the biopsy, and the laboratory. He added that I would need "no further therapy." I wasn't sure what he meant, so I asked, "You mean I won't have to do anything more in the future?"

He repeated, "You will need no further therapy," kind of mysteriously, I thought. I didn't have a clue what he meant, so I just paid the damn bill and left, hoping my insurance covered it.

When we got back to the clinic, I told Dr. Jacob what had happened. She called my doctor to get to the bottom of it and found out what had happened. Apparently, during the procedure he had used a special kind of new ultraviolet light that can detect precisely the area of the abnormal cells. There was only a small, isolated area, and he was able to burn it out with the laser, which is what he meant when he said "no further therapy." So basically, he either didn't understand that I didn't want to do the laser treatment . . . or just plain ignored me. Either way, it was done, and I couldn't freak out about it. Dr. Jacob was really excited about it and said I was very lucky. I was so happy and relieved. Farrah and I were practically jumping for joy.

◈ *June 4, 2008*

I just had one of those moments where your life changes in a flash. This morning I was getting ready to go with Farrah for her biopsy, not having slept well even after taking three Ativan, when Dr. Jacob came into my room with her medical chart.

She said, "Alana, come and sit," motioning me to sit on the bed across from her. "We must talk," she continued. "I have some news from Dr. Phutzenreuter. There is good news, and some not so good news. The first biopsy came back from the tissue he lasered out, and it is stage one cancer."

It happened so quickly and unexpectedly that I don't remember what I said. Probably "Are you kidding?" As if this would be a joke. I suddenly heard Farrah's voice in my head as I remembered what she had said to her doctors when they told her she had cancer: "No, I *don't*. I couldn't have cancer!" My reaction was the same. Total and complete denial that this could be happening to me.

Dr. Jacob continued: "The good news, Alana, is that he's fairly certain he removed it all. Now, we will know for sure when the rest of the biopsy report comes back. If there are any cancer cells in the surrounding tissue, then you will have to go back and he will remove them. It's a very good thing you went yesterday. You are lucky."

I didn't feel lucky—or even scared. Just kind of practical and businesslike. "How do we know it isn't anywhere else?" I asked.

"We could do a PET scan. In fact, we probably should," she replied.

"Yes, let's do it right away. Body and brain? Do I still have to go to Stuttgart?" The trip from hell.

"Yes, they're still the best," she replied.

"Okay. The sooner the better. I don't want to sit around on pins and needles."

"And now I will take some blood to check your tumor markers and we will send it to Greece for a vaccine. I'm sorry, Alana, but it's better to know now when it's so early and maybe he has already gotten it all."

I went straight into Farrah's room to tell her, but Dr. Jacob had beat me to it. When I walked in, Farrah was completely in shock. She hugged me and said, "Don't worry. It's going to be okay."

I replied, "It better be. Otherwise, you're going to have to get well quick so you can take care of *me*."

**Later**

Dr. Jacob came in with all my blood work results and the report from Dr. Rotorooter. The tissue around the area was negative. No cancer cells. She reiterated how lucky I was to have gone right away and that they found it so early. I felt pretty paranoid, so I asked if I should go back and get the rest of it burned out, but she said that wasn't necessary because the rest of the tissue was cancer free. I just had to put it out of my mind for now. Almost like it hadn't happened.

Now I'm lying on the other bed in Farrah's room while she's in surgery. They're doing a deep biopsy of the anal area where the primary tumor was, and hopefully there will be no new growth or cancer cells. If there are, then Dr. Kiehling said he will have to remove it, but very carefully because it's so close to the sphincter muscle.

This all seems like a dream and not a good one. To be going through all this with Farrah and find out I have cancer, too? But it was just a few cells in the cervix and they're gone now, right? Do you spell cancer and cervix with a capital *C*? I don't like giving

cancer that much importance. It's so odd. All my life I've been terrified of cancer, and now I find out I have or, if I'm lucky, had it. I
feel kind of numb, but not particularly scared, as if it isn't even
real. Anyway, I can't have cancer; I have too much to do.

### ◈ June 5, 2008

It's 3:30 A.M. and I've been awake for an hour, lying here in the
dark, thinking . . . thinking . . . The tears have finally come. I'm
confused and scared. Is this a wake-up call to stop living in fear,
embrace my life, and enjoy every moment?

I can't continue to live in this fear of the future: what's going to
happen when I run out of money? . . . how can I bear the pain of
seeing my children struggle? . . . having watched my two sons almost kill themselves with drugs . . . seeing Sean's frustration and
pain and anger because of his disabilities and because of his relationship with his father . . . seeing my best friend suffer so much
these past two years as she battles a tenacious, aggressive cancer . . .
not knowing if she's going to win this battle in the end.

I know I have a choice—to be a poor victim and run away
from life or go forward with faith and confidence and still do
something useful in the world. I forget I'm shooting this documentary with Farrah and she's just made a deal with NBC to air
it. So that's no small feat. Maybe it will inspire and educate a lot of
people and even save lives. I need to get off myself and thank God
for all these blessings. Maybe I should try to shift my attitude and
see the glass as half full, see the things I have to be grateful for.

Come on! Get off the pity pot and "be the fabulous woman you were meant to be," as Marianne says. This is just another bump on the road.

*God, give me the will and enthusiasm to live this life and let me find the joy and happiness in it. Let me start seeing that glass as half full, even three-quarters full. Change my perception of my life, myself, my kids. Show me what you would have me do to be a light in the world, God, and walk with me each step of the way. Heal me completely, Father, that I might be an example, and let me be the woman you would have me be in order to do what you would have me do.*

*And heal my sister Farrah in body, mind, and spirit that she might also be the woman you would have her be and give hope and inspiration to others.*

*Thank you, God.*

*Amen*

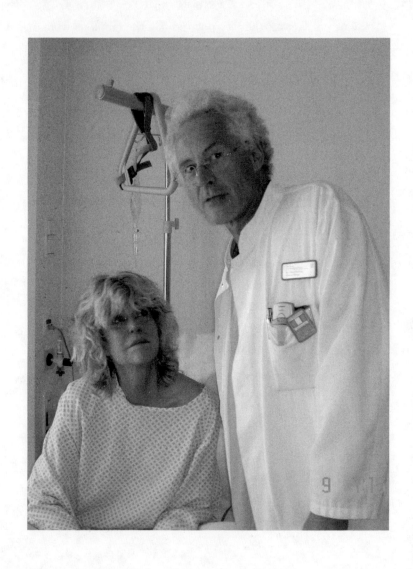

For a man who deals with deadly disease on a daily basis, Dr. Kiehling is one happy fella. We met him in May 2007 during Farrah's first trip to Germany. Farrah affectionately referred to him as "the mad scientist" because he was always laughing and smiling.

Perhaps it was his kind and humorous demeanor, but at first we weren't quite sure what to make of him. We'd been told that he could do what no other surgeon in the States had suggested: remove Farrah's anal tumor with ultrasound surgery. The tissue around it had been so badly damaged from the radiation that none of her doctors seemed willing to try this approach. But Dr. Jacob said she knew a surgeon who could do it, and in walked Dr. Kiehling. With an introduction like that, I think that both Farrah and I were expecting someone a little more serious and intense. Instead, Kiehling was warm, friendly, and jovial and was soon chatting with Farrah as if they were old friends.

"We will remove your tumor, yes?" he said, beaming. "It will be hard, but I have done this before."

The reassurance and confidence in his voice were very different from what we were hearing from other people. His attitude was so upbeat and positive that it matched Farrah's own outlook perfectly. She believed she had found the best person for the job.

◈ *June 6, 2008*

Another day of shocking news. Farrah's biopsy came back and she *does* have another malignant tumor in the primary area. The doctor said it's deeper than the other one, and the surgery will probably take a little longer than the one a year ago. I think we both sort of knew it, but hoped it wasn't true. It was a real blow to her.

I put my arms around her and we both cried.

"I just don't want to give up hope," she said through her tears.

There wasn't much I could say. She'd been through so much, and now she was facing yet another surgery on Monday. So I just held her close. "I'm so sorry," I whispered. "But you can't give up hope. You've come too far."

Then the phone rang. It was her dad. She started crying when she told him, and I felt my own tears welling up again. Her dad, her pillar of strength, was listening to his only surviving daughter tell him the bad news.

Why, I wondered, was this happening to Farrah? Is there a lesson in all of this? I think there's always a cause underneath any disease. Many spiritual teachers believe that all illness has a correlating mental equivalent. Louise Hay puts it succinctly: "when we create peace and harmony and balance in our minds, we will find it in our lives." That makes so much sense . . . it's just not easy to do.

I went back to my room, where I opened an e-mail from George. He said he was still shocked by my news about the cervical cancer, but it was good they got it so early. I e-mailed him back that I felt like I'd never really had it because by the time I knew I had it, it was gone. Cancer for a day. I said I figured the worst that could happen was I could die. At least I wouldn't have to worry about being old and broke!

## June 8, 2008

Neither Farrah nor I feel great today. Last night she started the thalidomide pills that are supposed to inhibit the cancer cells from growing. It's the same thalidomide that caused all the birth defects in the sixties, and they're now using it on certain fast-growing tumors. She had a couple of other shots today as well, and I woke up, after not sleeping well again, with my throat still sore. Also, I started bleeding from the surgery site, which made me nervous. What a pair we are.

"I liked it better when you were well and taking care of me," she joked.

"You better get well, because the tables may turn soon," I retorted. Bite my tongue.

My astrologer doesn't like the date for Farrah's surgery tomorrow. Mercury is still in retrograde and she says it's possible she will have to repeat the surgery. She'd like her to wait until next Wednesday, but Farrah wants to go ahead with it. She just wants it out. I know if it were me, I'd wait the two days, but it's her decision. And we know how stubborn she can be. My theory is, the more things you have on your side—even the stars—the better.

The weather is so chilly and gloomy today. It's rained nearly every day since we've been here. I felt pretty good when we arrived, but now it's getting really depressing. Even the weather is pessimistic. I feel like if we could just look out on those hills and see a ray of sunshine, it would be enough to lift our spirits. But no such luck. Maybe tomorrow.

I was supposed to have dinner with Mimmo tonight, but he called to say he was going to watch the Formula One race on television instead. I was waiting for him to invite me over, but he didn't. Actually, it's a relief, because I feel sick, but it's a perfect example of his self-centeredness. I have to say, it's starting to annoy me.

❖ *June 9, 2008*

The taxi brought us to the hospital in the little town of Bad Tölz at nine thirty in the morning. At ten forty-five we were still waiting for them to come get her for the surgery. The hospitals in Germany, at least the ones we've seen, are much nicer and more comfortable than any hospital in Los Angeles. Everything looks new and clean. The language barrier is the only problem, but even so, the nurses and doctors all try very hard to accommodate us. They've given Farrah a sedative to relax her and she's fallen asleep.

We talked on the way over. She told me she'd asked Dr. Jacob what the prognosis is now that the tumors' resistance to the anti-cancer drugs has gone up to 80 percent. She also asked if anybody had ever survived this particular cancer. Dr. Jacob said no. I know that inside, Farrah has to be sad and frightened by this statement—knowing that, without a miracle, there would be no happy ending. But neither one of us voiced it. She's still determined not to give up—and so am I.

Shortly after Farrah's surgery, I went down to the recovery room to see her, and I found her surprisingly alert. She was still a little stoned from the medication and had me in stitches. The Germans in the cubicle next to us were talking so loudly that they could have been in a beer garden or at a soccer match. I think that's the only way they know how to talk. Farrah kept yelling at them to shut up and kept trying to get up and go back to her room, despite the fact that she was hooked up to monitors. I was afraid she was going to pull them out of the wall!

I walked into the little village to get some strudel, the only German dessert we like. Even though she'd just had a major operation, Farrah was ready to eat and asked me to bring some back for her. For the first day since we've been here, the sun was out, and everything was radiantly green and vivid. Beautiful flowers were blooming everywhere and the smell of freshly cut grass was in the air. After all the terrible weather, I felt hopeful and happy to be out in the fresh air, walking around the little town.

◈ *June 10, 2008*

Where do I start? Everything seems to be coming at us so fast and furious that I can barely keep my head above water. Dr. Kiehling, who had performed the surgery, came into the hospital room around 4 P.M. on Monday afternoon, and from the look on his face I knew it wasn't good news. His expression was so sad and so compassionate that I thought he was going to tell Farrah she was going to die tomorrow. She braced herself. Then he began to speak.

"The tumor is larger than I expected and in a very precarious position. I need to do another surgery in the next couple of days."

Farrah started crying, and he put his arms around her and held her close. Before long, she was laughing and joking with him. She's truly incredible. I don't know how she is maintaining such a strong spirit and attitude. Most people would have crumbled. But she rallies. She picks herself up, dusts herself off, and goes on fighting.

I've been joking about my own brush with cancer, my "cancer for a day." Let's hope it's only a brush. I still have to do the PET scan to make sure it hasn't spread to the lymph or anywhere else. Part of me feels sure it hasn't, but after all this, God only knows. Deep down I'm scared. I don't really believe it's anywhere else, but then, I didn't believe this would happen to Farrah, either.

Dr. Jacob came in and said that even with this new setback she feels very hopeful because there are some new antibodies, available only recently, that have tested very strongly against Farrah's kind of cancer. This is the most impressive thing about Germany. They're using these cutting-edge treatments years before the States. It seems like the FDA and all the rules and regulations keep us far behind them. What I've seen here is eye-opening.

Dr. Jacob said she feels very positive about Farrah's chances now. She was very honest. She said, "Farrah, I will never give you false hope, but I will never give up on you, either." This made Farrah smile. We had planned on staying at the hospital that night, but Farrah said she was feeling fine and wanted to go back to the clinic, so Dr. Jacob drove us.

Back at the clinic, we sat up talking until one thirty in the morning. It felt just like the old days, when we used to sit on the phone for hours, talking away about anything and everything. Farrah read me an entry from her journal that she'd just finished. She'd never shared her writing with me before. It was very touching, so honest and from her heart. She said, almost apologetically, "My writing's not nearly as good as yours."

"Are you crazy?" I said. "You don't have any idea how beautiful this is. It's so descriptive and so poetic. This has to be the narrative running through the documentary. It's so powerful." She was talking about life and how fragile and fleeting it can be. She'd been hit by so many blows, one after the other. One phrase particularly stayed with me: "They can keep cutting out parts of me, but they can't cut out my spirit. Sometimes I feel like a blond nothingness."

Later, as I lay in my bed, I couldn't sleep, thinking about the past few days . . . the past year. How did we get here, my friend? You are in this life-threatening battle with cancer, and I'm going through it with you. Then I had this cancer scare myself. I feel like my entire concept of what it means to be there for someone is changing. Supporting Farrah through this has been an exercise in constant motion, never having enough time or space to find my feet before the ground disappears beneath them again. It's been a nonstop game of catch-up with my emotions. I constantly have the sensation that we're hurtling through space, faster than the speed of light, and I don't have time to digest or process anything. This has been one of the hardest things I've ever done in my life. I feel like I just have to hold on and try not to go under while the raging current sweeps us along.

*June 11, 2008*

Okay, God, enough is enough! I am so sick that I'm barely able to swallow. Dr. Jacob did a swab of my throat and she thinks I have strep but has to wait for the results to know what antibiotics work on this particular strain. Fortunately, she was able to move Farrah's surgery to Thursday. There was no way I could have made it today to help take care of her, besides the fact that she doesn't need to be around my germs.

What if I can't go with Farrah tomorrow for her surgery? She'll have to be in the hospital three days this time. It's a serious operation. I don't have time to be sick.

**Later**

Finally, some good news! Dr. Jacob came into my room with the lab reports: there's no cancer in my blood, and the tumor markers are normal. She said that means the cancer was localized and the doctor got it all. Thank you, God! I still have to do the PET scan to make 100 percent sure it's not in my lymph or anywhere else, but she doesn't think it will be. She started me right away on an IV of antibiotics to knock out my throat infection. I feel better already, just knowing that everything looks much more positive.

I asked her about Farrah's operation tomorrow. Would it be terribly painful? She said that it would not, and that she will only be in the hospital two days. Please, God, let this turn around.

*June 12, 2008*

Farrah's surgery day. We got to the hospital early, around 9 A.M., and of course waited and waited. Apparently the doctor was running late with other surgeries. Finally, they came to prepare her. She looked frail and nervous, clutching her rosary, as they wheeled her into the operating room. I went with her as far as they would let me, before saying good-bye. She looked like a small, frightened child.

I'm sitting in the Schlössel (which means castle), a Bavarian restaurant down the road from the hospital, having some lunch and waiting for Farrah to come out of surgery. Please, God, let Dr. Kiehling come into the room with good news—that it went well, that they got the rest of the tumor, that it was easier than expected.

This restaurant is really depressing. It's the road show version of what one would imagine a German castle to be. Besides me, there's only one old German couple in here. What they're eating looks really good—sauerkraut and some kind of big dumplings. I'd probably have gas for two days. I couldn't read a word of the menu, so the woman tried to explain it in the few words of English she could speak. I really wanted sausages and sauerkraut, but I settled for fish. I'm not even hungry, just trying to pass the time. They just brought the fish. It's the size of a small whale.

I'm sitting here eating, feeling tears well up in my eyes. It's such a dreary, depressing day. Will the sun ever come back to Bavaria for more than a day? Will it ever come back into Farrah's life and mine? Funny, as I'm writing this the sun is just trying to break through the clouds, maybe for the third time in two weeks. Everything looks brighter—the trees, the grass, the sky. Perhaps it's a sign from God that it's all going to turn around. I know I need to be positive—to be strong for both of us. But I just feel so damned sad. I guess anyone would.

Farrah came back to the hospital room around three. I expected her to be much worse than she was. She didn't even seem to be in terrible pain but obviously was still being given a lot of drugs. Within a couple of hours, she was hungry. I went out to buy strudel, but the little pastry shop was closed on Thursdays. So I went back to the Schlössel and got some second-rate strudel there. We scarfed it down with tea and spent the rest of the evening trying to find something edible for dinner. They seem to be big on bread and cheese here in the hospital.

As always, I was blown away by Farrah's recuperative powers. Although she was a little slurry from the pain medication, we were filming, laughing, and joking about the food and the mean nurse, who of course didn't speak one word of English. Which is a good thing, considering the names we were calling her. It looked like Farrah was going to drop-kick the nurse when she tried to touch her. Though she's been so upbeat, I know there are days when she must doubt her faith and get angry with God for letting this happen to her. She always tries to see the greater good in her going through this, but there are moments, like this one, when her faith is pushed to the limits. If it were me, I'd probably be ripping people's heads off.

### June 14, 2008

Another gray day. I slept in the hospital with Farrah, and we actually managed to sleep from midnight till 10 A.M., an unheard-of feat in a hospital, where they usually come cheerily in around 5 A.M. and wake you up. I put a sign on the door last night saying "Do Not Disturb" in every language I could think of. I guess "Verboten" did it, because not a soul bothered us.

Farrah woke up in a lot of pain, so I don't know if we'll go "home" today. Scary that I'm starting to think of the clinic as home. I think I'll go crazy if we don't get out of this hospital soon.

This week has passed so fast I've hardly thought about Mimmo. I feel he really cares about me, but I'm pretty sure he puts himself, along with his fitness, his tanning, his pedicures, and his biking, before me. When I told him about my cancer, he didn't seem to have much of a reaction, which surprised me. After all, it's cancer, not a hangnail. We never talked about it again, and it left me feeling let down and disappointed. And he hasn't been begging to come and sit by my bedside this past week when I've been so sick. Maybe all men are like this—certainly a lot of the ones I've known are, especially when it comes to "female problems." As long as you're up, fun, looking great, and sexy, they're right there. But when you're down, I'm not sure a lot of them really know how to show up for you. That's where your girlfriends come in. They'll hold your hand when you're crying and your head when you're throwing up.

When I think about it, my friendship with Farrah has outlasted any of my relationships with men. I have never survived thirty years with one guy—and frankly, I'm not sure I could. And even more incredible is that during those thirty years, we've only fought twice—both times over her being late for a flight.


◈ *June 15, 2008*


Tonight, Farrah and I watched a documentary called *The Heart of Healing*. It's about cancer and different diseases and what a huge role the subconscious mind plays in healing. According to the documentary, our emotions have a great impact on our immune system, and when we get angry or upset or scared, our adrenaline goes right down to the lymph, where our killer cells hang out. God, my killer cells must all be wearing helmets! Farrah was fascinated with the message of the documentary. This whole experience with cancer has made her realize how much stress has impacted her health. I've seen her make a conscious effort to keep stress at a minimum in her life. I don't know if there is one golden rule on how to do this—we all have to find our own way. For me, a lot of it has to do with putting everything in its proper perspective. Sometimes it's as simple as taking a deep breath and asking myself, "How important is this to me? Is it worth getting myself upset over? How much does it matter?" Sometimes you just have to "let go and let God."

### June 17, 2008

I was in Farrah's room with her and Dr. Jacob today, having a competition about cancer. We've both developed a bizarre and morbid sense of humor during all of this.

"Well, you only had cancer for a day," Farrah said.

"So?" I replied. "That still makes me a cancer survivor, right?" I looked at Dr. Jacob for confirmation.

"We don't know yet," the doctor said, and laughed that hearty laugh of hers.

"Oh, great. Thanks a lot," I said. We were all laughing at the time, but afterward, when Dr. Jacob and I were in my room alone, I brought up the subject again.

"I thought it was gone. They got it all, right?" I asked.

"Alana, there is never a guarantee it won't come back. You have to be checked very carefully from now on. You should also have an ultrasound of your kidneys and liver every six months.

You have all these latent viruses, and your immune function is lowered. Your killer cell count is half of what it should be. You have to take care."

Now I'm feeling an icy fear in my chest. "Do you think the PET scan will be okay?" I asked.

"Yes, I think so. Now don't worry," she admonished as she left the room. But she could see the look of anxiety on my face. "It's normal to feel this way," she said. "You're still in shock. First, going through all this with Farrah, and then finding out about your own brush with cancer."

I hadn't been able to cry in weeks, and suddenly I started weeping. She said it was good for me not to hold it in.

"And Sean," I sobbed through my tears. "He doesn't feel well. He says he feels weak all the time. He said the only time he feels good is when he's here."

"Alana," she said, "it's his brain. And he must not do drugs or alcohol."

"Even when he's sober, he still has problems focusing and says that his body feels weak." I was sobbing so hard I could barely get my words out. "Can he get better?"

"Yes," she said. "The stem cells repair his brain, but when he drinks or does drugs, it destroys them."

I tell her I'm worried about Ashley, too, all the years he used drugs.

"Alana, your children are grown. You have to think about yourself now."

"But I love them so much. I don't want anything to happen to them," I managed to get out through the tears.

"Your children will be okay. You must not worry so much," she said gently, patting my hand.

Easy to say. I tell her I'm worried about my kids, I'm worried about myself, and I'm worried about Farrah. Life just feels hopeless.

"It's not hopeless at all, Alana. And there is hope for Farrah, too. We are doing all these new treatments, and I really do think this new trial chemo program with Dr. Forman in Los Angeles can help her." Then she left, saying she would give me a natural medicine that would help calm the circus of emotions inside me.

I cried a little more and felt much better. I've probably needed a good cry for a long time now. I can even take a deep breath now, which I haven't been able to do in months.

**Later**

Mimmo called around five and I said I would come over for dinner at seven thirty. I was running late and didn't get there until eight thirty. He was working feverishly in the kitchen. The restaurant was packed, but he'd saved the first banquette, where I always sit, for me.

As I sat alone in his beautiful, romantic, candle-lit restaurant, I started to feel deeply sad. I'd come back to Germany thinking it was going to be like the last two times with Mimmo, but this trip has been different. Before, our relationship was romantic and sexy and lighthearted. Now, it's . . . I don't know exactly. Sad, I guess. Just sad.

He joined me and ate his dinner. He showed me his new cell phone and told me about the new five-hundred-Euro bicycle he'd bought today. I wonder if he spoke English or if my Italian was more fluent, would the conversation be so superficial? Sadly, I fear it would.

As the conversation progressed, we began to talk about Sean, and Mimmo was saying how much Sean loves me. I said it was a pity Mimmo and his mother weren't close. He's told me before how they always clashed and that his *nonna* (grandmother) was more like a mother to him.

"Psychologists," I said to him, "say that men who don't have good relationships with their mothers have problems in relationships with women."

"I don't have problems. I have had a lot of relationships," he said.

"That's my point," I countered. "Lots, maybe, but none lasting."

"Women are too difficult," he said. "They always want to know where you are, what you're doing, who you've talked to."

I told him, jokingly but meaning it, that that was because he's selfish. *Egoista* in Italian. He always does what he wants, when he wants.

"When you're at my house in L.A., I ask you every day what you want to do," I said. "I don't just go off and do things alone."

He said, "But I always do everything you ask me to do when you're here. When have I ever said no to anything?"

"But I never ask you to do anything!" I countered.

"But I would, though."

"Okay," I said, knowing full well he was looking forward to a sunny Sunday so he could go ride his new bike in the mountains all day. "Farrah and I would love to go to the lake on Sunday." I smiled sweetly.

"Well, I will, if you really want to," he said, trying to mean it, but looking like he was being asked to sacrifice his right arm.

"You'd die!" I said, laughing.

"Well," he said sheepishly, "what about Saturday afternoon?"

I just laughed again. I'd made my point.

I was going to walk back to the clinic, but he insisted on driving me. He'd even prepared food for me to take to Farrah. Outside, walking to the car, he stopped me and asked, *"Potete darmi un bacio?"* (Can you give me a kiss?) Then, "You don't kiss me anymore."

When I got out of the car at the clinic, I kissed him on the cheek and thanked him for dinner and for Farrah's food. Heading back into the clinic, I found that feeling of sadness creeping back in. I stopped by Farrah's room, and we talked while she ate. I told her what had happened and she listened thoughtfully.

"I'm not sure he's mentally stimulating enough for me," I said. "Maybe it's the language barrier, but even so, how much time can you spend talking about cell phones and bicycles?"

Just talking it over with Farrah was helpful, but I think both of us are beginning to think this relationship has possibly run its course.

### June 18, 2008

We were supposed to be coming home to L.A. today. Now it looks like we'll be here at least another week, if not more. Dr. Jacob just told me that Farrah has been really sick all night. She started throwing up at 4 A.M. and it continued on for hours. She's finally sleeping now.

I remember Dr. Jacob saying to me the other day that there was always the possibility of an unexpected setback if some kind of complication or infection occurred. That's always in the back of my mind now.

**Later**

Cancer is the great leveler of humanity. It doesn't care if you're a superstar or a housemaid. Everyone suffers the same indignities, although it must be a great plus if one has the money to afford the best doctors and the best care.

I've seen it now, up close and personal, and it's not pretty . . . not easy. Farrah has been so ill today; she's terribly weak and in pain. Everything seemed to be going well yesterday. She was her feisty self—doing business on the phone, giving the people here at the clinic hell (but with good reason). We were up late, talking and laughing, just like the old days. Then she got so ill in the night. I wish she'd called me. The nurses were with her, but still, she shouldn't have gone through it alone.

We won't leave for Frankfurt tomorrow, that's for sure. Friday is Dr. Vogl's last day before he leaves for his vacation, and Dr. Jacob and he feel it's essential she have the liver perfusion. I don't see how she can handle much more. This has been too much for one body to take.

*The Three Musketeers.*

*Tina Sinatra and I have been best of friends since I first moved to L.A. In the beginning of our relationship, when my mother died, she showed up at the funeral to support me, and we've been best friends ever since. I introduced her to Farrah, though I can't remember exactly when. All I know is that we just clicked from the beginning. We were all so different, but we brought out the best in one another since day one.*

*We had this tradition—every time we were together, we had to take a photo. Tina always says she's hidden behind our big Texas blond hair, which Farrah and I took great pleasure in doing intentionally! This shot was taken at Christmas in 1991. We shared a lot of fun times together: birthdays, holidays, parties, and just intimate dinners at one of our houses. Tina has the biggest heart in the world. She is the kind of gal you love having as a friend . . . but would hate to have as an enemy.*

# ONE DAY AT A TIME

———⬥———

◈ *June 19, 2008*

Farrah definitely can't travel today. She's still too weak. This morning, for the first time, I felt her determination starting to slip.

"I was thinking earlier that I wasn't going to make it this time," she confessed to me. "I have just never suffered as much as these last two days."

I did my best cheerleading. "Of course you're going to make it. We just have to take it a day at a time."

Truthfully, I'm worried about the trip to Frankfurt for the liver perfusion. To travel five or six hours in a car in her weakened state and go through another surgical procedure is asking a lot. She's so weak she's having trouble just walking to the bathroom. I know Dr. Vogl and Dr. Jacob both feel she must have this second perfusion to continue to shrink the tumors in her liver. Dr. Jacob is more worried about the liver than anything else and feels it's essential for Farrah to have it. I suggested we take a nurse with us, and Dr. Vogl seconded the idea. We'll have to see how she is tonight.

I can't believe Dr. Jacob left for a conference and isn't here all day. She is so busy, and as a result I have to make important decisions for Farrah without any medical advisement. And we're here in a country where we don't speak the language. This is crazy. I feel like I'm in over my head—a child trying to do something she's not equipped to do. This is all new to me. I sometimes feel like there's no one to drive this stagecoach and it's getting out of control. But having said all that, I know I'm strong and I have to help her through this. No one could go through this alone. You have to have someone there all the time, fighting for you.

◈ *June 20, 2008*

We're on our way to Frankfurt after all. Dr. Jacob finally came in this morning and spoke to Dr. Vogl again. The only choice now is to go today or wait for almost three weeks. Dr. Jacob also talked to Dr. Forman at City of Hope in Los Angeles last night, after we coordinated the phone call and insisted they speak. He's going to try to get Farrah into a trial of a new cancer treatment that both he and Dr. Jacob think could be very beneficial for her. She couldn't start right away, however, so he was also in favor of her going to Dr. Vogl if she can make it.

Farrah decided to go for it. She's so weak and in so much pain, she can hardly walk. At my insistence, they finally found a nurse to come with us. I told Dr. Jacob that, with Farrah in this condition, they couldn't just send us on a five-hour trip on the autobahn, not speaking a word of German. Like a medevac Thelma and Louise!

At the moment, we're a couple of hours away from Frankfurt, and Farrah is sleeping. I've had to delay my PET scan until Tuesday. I'm a little nervous about it. God forbid they find anything. I need to get my thinking straight. I want to live, I really do, although I don't think I could go through what I've seen Farrah go through this past year and a half.

**Later**

Thelma and Louise are back on the road again—the long drive back to the clinic. Fortunately, it was all a success. Dr. Vogl said the tumors had shrunk 30 percent from last time, which he was very pleased about. Thank God we came, and thank God for Dr. Vogl.

I'm so exhausted that I can't wait to get into bed. Unfortunately, I won't be getting into my own bed. I slept in Farrah's room last night because I've got this horrible, musty odor in my room. I'm convinced it's mold and it's slowly killing me. The housekeeper thinks I'm crazy. I've had every piece of upholstered furniture taken out of the room. She couldn't smell the odor, although Farrah smelled it immediately, and so did the night nurse. Finally, I dragged Dr. Jacob in this morning and she smelled it, too. I kept thinking maybe I was crazy or neurotic, and didn't want to be any more of a pain in the ass than I've already been, but after sleeping in Farrah's room last night, I felt much better.

Dr. Jacob said that the room next to me will be free on Sunday. I'll sleep in Farrah's room until then. It feels a little like a slumber party. Farrah said, "I like you sleeping in my room. You should just move in."

"I'd love to," I said, "but I don't think we could fit all our clothes."

### June 21, 2008

Good news! Dr. Jacob came into Farrah's room this morning very excited. She spoke to Dr. Vogl late last night. He'd just reviewed the scans and said that Farrah's tumors had shrunk more than he'd originally thought. More than 50 percent, which he said was "amazing, better than anyone had ever reacted from one perfusion." Dr. Jacob said the new treatment regimen has helped turn things around, and that the vaccines she's now giving Farrah are changing the genetic makeup of the tumors and helping to destroy them. She feels much more positive about Farrah's progress and is quite hopeful now. She was so happy that she had tears in her eyes. It's great to have some good news after these very difficult four weeks.

We're leaving on Friday, but I'm worried that when Farrah gets back to Los Angeles she will try to jump right into editing the documentary for NBC. I don't want her to put too much pressure and stress on herself at a time when she desperately needs to focus on healing. But when her mind is made up about something, it's tough if not impossible to stop her, so I'll probably have to let it go.

This is where I have to detach from people I care about. I can't make myself feel responsible for their decisions about their health or anything else. I have to be there as much as I can, be an advocate when it's needed, and be a supportive friend, but I can't control the decisions they make or the resulting outcome. It's the same with my kids. I watch them make decisions that I know are going to have negative results, and eventually when that happens, they come to me, and it causes me pain to see them suffer. In the end, though, they are making their own choices.

### June 22, 2008

I'm sitting on the terrace outside Farrah's room, waiting to move into my new room. The musty odor in my room has gotten so bad now that all the doctors can smell it and they agree there is definitely something there. I'm in a state of paranoia about it. Farrah and I have dubbed it "the mold suite."

Farrah is sleeping now. She was in such horrible pain that Dr. Jacob came in and gave her a pain IV. All she could do was just lie there and sob. God, it breaks my heart to see her in such pain. There's nothing I can do but be there—and that makes me feel helpless. I can only try and comfort her and assure her that it will be better soon. Just hang in . . .

Farrah and I went to Mimmo's last night for dinner. I was afraid it would be too much for her, but she really wanted to go. Speaking of Mimmo, I was so pissed at him I barely spoke to him. He had called earlier and said there was a big soccer match on Sunday night, so he wouldn't be able to take Farrah and me to dinner. It reminded me of Rod when we were married. Mimmo goes bicycling all day on Sunday whether I'm here or not, and when Rod and I were married, he played soccer all day every Sunday and then went to the pub with the boys afterward for hours. He'd always come home late for Sunday dinner, which by that time would be stone cold, but not as cold as me. It wouldn't have been such a big deal except that Sunday was the only day he had to spend with me and the kids because he was in the studio all week.

It became a big issue in our marriage. Now, I look back and think, "Why did I let it bother me so much? Why didn't I just let him do what made him happy and not take it so personally?" I always end up with men who are completely self-centered and then try to change them, and when I can't, I get angry at them. I end up feeling, in some way, that they don't care enough about me and are not making me a priority in their life. Since this has happened with every man in my life, I think I'd better look at myself and my part in it. Funny how history—or at least my history—repeats itself.

I really have to remember that things always work out for the best if you just let go and don't try to control them or take them personally. God, do I need another thirty years in therapy to figure it all out? By then I'll be ninety and too old to care.

 

◈ *June 23, 2008*

Farrah was so sick last night, I was afraid she would go into one of those all-night marathons of vomiting. I'm not sure what the record is now. Ryan swears it was the night he went with her to Frankfurt for Dr. Vogl's perfusion, and she threw up for six hours in the van all the way back to the clinic. I still think the record is that seventy-five times in twelve hours, again in Frankfurt.

There was only one nurse here last night. She doesn't speak

English very well and Dr. Jacob was away in Frankfurt. Farrah finally went to sleep, thank God. I slept in her room in case she got sick again.

Today was a brighter day. Now if we can just get our room situation sorted out. I'm starting to smell that musty odor in my new room, which is next to "the mold suite," and in Farrah's room as well. They may think I'm crazy, but I know mold when I smell it. Farrah said last night, in the midst of her pain, "We've got to get out of here. They're trying to kill us." Well, it is starting to feel that way!

And on top of everything else, I have to go to Stuttgart tomorrow for my PET scan. The doctor reads the results to me right afterward. What if they find something and I'm there alone? I know I have to think positively, but there's been so much shocking, unexpected news on this trip that I'm a little gun-shy.

### June 24, 2008

I'm on my way to Stuttgart for the PET scan. I can't believe that June is almost over. I barely remember it. The surgeries, the doctors, the hospitals and clinics have all blended together into one dreary, wet, German blur. We've been hoping to get out and do some filming by the lake or in the mountains. There are so many beautiful places around here in Bavaria, but we haven't been able to make it. We thought for sure we'd be going home this week, but Farrah doesn't seem to be getting better fast enough.

Farrah would have come with me for the scan, but she's just too sick. She had a terrible night. At midnight, just as I was going to sleep, the nurse called me to say that Farrah had started throwing up again and was in terrible pain. They gave her all the right things, but nothing was working. I'd taken an Ativan and could barely keep my eyes open, but I stayed in her room with her. I ended up sleeping there. Every time I'd drift off to sleep, I'd wake up a few minutes later when she would start throwing up again. Finally, the doctor gave her a shot that put her to sleep and I was able to get a few hours of sleep myself.

Now it's raining cats and dogs, accompanied by thunder and lightning that seem frighteningly close. God, please, just let us get back to sunny California. I feel very alone right now. Alone and scared.

**Later 2:20 P.M.**

I just finished the PET scan and I'm sitting in the office, waiting for Dr. Horr to give me his report. I wasn't allowed to eat all day and I'm hungry, weak, and nervous. I'm wolfing down a banana and wishing there were something more to eat here. He's calling me in now. Boy, is my heart pounding!

"Sit down." He gestures to a chair in front of several computer screens lit up with slides of my body and brain.

"So, do I have any tumors?" I blurt out. I can't wait any longer to know.

"No, no, you are fine," he says matter-of-factly, not realizing that he's just told me I still have a life to live. Thank you, God, thank you, thank you, thank you! I'll never complain again, I swear it!

**Later 6:30 P.M.**

I just left Dr. Rotorooter's office in Munich. I wanted to get it all over with in one day. Gynecologists are really different here. First of all, there's no nurse in the room when they examine you. He had me take off my clothes from the waist down and lean back in this large chair with my legs in stirrups, up in the air and wide apart. No sheet, nada. When he finished examining me, he sat back, took off his gloves, and proceeded to talk to me while I remained in the same spread-eagle position. All the while he was talking, I was wishing I had the camera and could shoot him from my point of view, framed by my wide-apart legs.

The good news was that everything had healed well. I then asked nervously if the cancer could come back. He said, as best as I could understand with his limited English, he had lasered the whole area and the surrounding tissue was cancer free. He added that I should still get Pap smears every few months. I guess I'll never get a Pap smear again without holding my breath for the results.

So, now that this major worry is over, I can get on with my life. But it's not the same life. How could it be? If this experience wasn't a wake-up call, then I don't know what is. I can now honestly say that I feel there's a Higher Power out there who wants me to live. Maybe it's so that I can be here for Farrah? I feel a deep sense of commitment to continuing this path with her, no matter where it might lead.

I started this journey with her, particularly the German part. I wanted her to come here because I thought they could help her. I felt she'd die if she stayed in the States, and now even some of the doctors there are admitting that she probably wouldn't be alive today if she hadn't come here. The first time she came, a year ago, I told her that I'd stay as long as she had to stay. After that, I felt like I had to come back with her because I knew the routine. I'm not being self-important; it was just a fact. I felt I had to stick by her.

I'm sure that a big part of it has to do with what happened with my grandmother and my mother. When my grandmother's colon cancer came back, years ago, I didn't try hard enough to make her go into Houston where there were better doctors. She didn't want to leave Nacogdoches and the local doctor there, so I didn't push it. At the time, a part of me may have even been relieved by her choice, because I didn't know any doctors in Houston and it seemed overwhelming. Then she died, minutes before I arrived at the hospital, and I never got to say good-bye to her. I was devastated, and even now it brings tears to my eyes that I didn't make more of an effort to spend time with her when she was alive. I've felt tremendous amounts of guilt about that ever since.

That guilt only got worse when, shortly after my grandmother's death, my mother died of an overdose of prescription drugs. Once again I did not get a chance to say good-bye, leaving me riddled with guilt that I hadn't done enough to save her.

So maybe, in some way, by doing this for Farrah, I'm atoning for the past when I didn't give my all, for times when I allowed myself to be distracted or caught up or when I lost sight of the connections, the people in life who really matter. That's why I've always gone the extra mile and more when it's come to trying to save my sons from their addictions. I know from years in Al-Anon that I can't "save" anyone, but if something happened to one of them and I hadn't done everything in my power to help them, I couldn't live with myself.

I don't have a lot to give materially to my friends, but I can give my friendship and my time. This whole experience has changed forever the way I value friendship. Would someone do this for me? I know Farrah would.

It reminds me of this lovely birthday card Farrah gave me last year that I keep in the drawer next to my bed. On the front it has these two little girls with pigtails, holding hands, walking barefoot on a dirt road. It says, "By my side, step by step . . . that is where you are for me, that is where I will be for you." On the inside she wrote the following:

*Dearest Alana, not only do I wish you the happiest healthiest birthday but I want to say thank you for your unbelievable friendship. You are my best friend forever and I appreciate you and all you've done and continue to do from the bottom of my heart. I love you, sweet girl, and you are, as my mother would say, as beautiful on the inside as you are on the outside.*

*All my love,*
*Farrah*

We called ourselves "The Do Nothing Girls."

In 2001 we went down to Don Soffer's big sprawling house in Harbour Island with our friend Nicollette Sheridan and my son Ash. Farrah and I did nothing but sleep late and lie around the pool (hence our nickname).

We took the Jeep one day because we wanted to drive down to the beach. When we got there, we walked along this beautiful deserted beach together, leaving our footprints in miles of pink sand. Farrah got the brilliant idea that she wanted to take the sand back to use in the sculptures she was doing for an exhibit at the Los Angeles County Museum of Art. We went back to the house, got large baggies, then went back to the beach and filled them with sand, but they were so damn heavy that we could barely lift them.

"I can't believe you're making me carry this!" I complained.

But I did. We kept walking with our bags of sand in our arms, lugging them all the way back to the house.

When we were packing to leave Harbour Island, Farrah loaded the bags of sand in a box to take with her. I knew this was a bad idea; it was like tempting fate with customs. But that's the thing about Farrah: when she decides she's going to do something, it's really hard to talk her out of it. Believe me I tried. In the end she won and the sand came with us.

We flew back with the sand on Don's private plane and landed in Miami to go through customs. Not surprisingly, when the customs officers got to the box of pink sand, there was much discussion and delay. The official finally asked, "Did you get it off a private beach?"

*We looked at each other and we didn't know what to say—we were afraid they'd arrest us if we said the wrong thing.*

*After a long pause, Farrah flashed the officials one of her brightest smiles: "Can you make that a multiple-choice answer?"*

*Sure enough, we got through just fine, the bags of pink sand sitting pretty in our suitcases.*

# HARD CHOICES

———◆———

I'm so stressed out! Why can't life be simple? Sean's friend and publicist, Lizzie Grubman, called and said that Sean had written this incredibly touching letter to read to me at his graduation from rehab on Sunday. It says I'm the most important person in his life and the most supportive. Lizzie said it made her cry and that I have to be there on Sunday, in Los Angeles. How can I do this? Farrah is having a terrible day, with pain and nausea. Dr. Jacob had to give her so much medication that she's been sleeping all day. How can I leave her? I was thinking that maybe, if I can get his show, *Celebrity Rehab,* to fly me home, I could come in for Sean's graduation on Sunday and come back on Monday. His manager is trying to get the show to pay for it. I'll know tomorrow. Am I crazy? Can I physically do this?

Right now, I'm torn between two people I love who both need me. I don't want to desert Farrah, and yet I don't want to disappoint Sean. He's really counting on my being there because originally we were coming home before now. I know he'll be crushed if I don't show up. But I'm also afraid that because Farrah relies on me so much, she'll feel very abandoned. I wasn't going to worry her until I got it sorted out. But at last, I shared my dilemma with her.

"If I go, I'll come straight back," I promised.

I could tell she was nervous about it, but she said, "Don't worry. If you need to go, I understand. It's your son." Of course she would understand because her own son, Redmond, means so much to her.

On top of it, Kim's going through a really rough time in London. She wants me to come there and be with her. Our big issue is that she's always felt I was there for the boys, with all their problems, and that she didn't get as much of my time or attention. And of course I feel terribly guilty because of it.

I sent her an e-mail saying that I know I can't change the past, but that I will try to be there for her now, in any way I can. I said that after I got home and got things straightened out there, I would go stay with her in London. I didn't mention that I might be going home for Sean's graduation. I know that would be another sore point. Once again she'll feel like I was there for him and not for her.

Now Dr. Jacob says that there's no way Farrah can travel before next Wednesday. I can't figure all this out and I've got knots in my stomach. I feel like I'm being pulled in every direction. I'm trying to be completely selfless here, but what do I do when everybody seems to need me at once?

### June 26, 2008

Farrah is somewhat better today. Dr. Jacob said she would stay with her over the weekend if I end up going, so that's a relief. I just got an e-mail from Sean's manager saying that the network and the producers won't pay for my travel. I wish I could handle situations like this without getting so stressed out. Making difficult decisions seems to affect my whole system to the extent that I can't think clearly. It feels like my brain is on the spin cycle of a washing machine. The thought of getting on a plane, flying all those hours, being jet-lagged, having to show up at the graduation ceremony, which may entail being there all day because they're filming it—it's overwhelming. Not to mention racing back to Germany to be with Farrah.

### June 27, 2008

By the time I went to bed last night, I was exhausted and practically in tears. I started to feel unwell again, obviously brought on by stress. I talked to Lizzie, and she said I just *had* to be there for Sean. Apparently his girlfriend Caleigh broke up with him because she thought he'd cheated on her with some girl on the show, and Ash won't do it, so I was the only one. I spoke to Sean and his manager, Prem, and said I'd be there. I booked a flight for Saturday, so I could make Sean's graduation ceremony on Sunday. So it was settled. I felt terrible about leaving Farrah, but I knew I had to be there for my son. I told Farrah I'd turn around and come straight back if Ryan or someone else couldn't come over to accompany her back.

Then I got an urgent e-mail from Sean's manager to please call him right away. It seems that the producers had just changed the graduation to Saturday afternoon, which made it completely impossible for me to get there. I told him there was no way I could change everything to leave today. I couldn't pack, check out of the clinic, and get to Munich in time for the plane. Besides that, there were no seats available. I felt terrible for Sean, but this was now out of my hands. It was the producers' fault that I wouldn't be there, not mine.

I called Sean in tears, and he seemed absolutely fine. He said, "Mom, I can't talk. I have to go arm-wrestle Rodney King." Then he put Rodney King on the phone with me. He's his room-mate on the show. Yes, the same Rodney King that caused the L.A. riots after he led the police on a high-speed chase and they beat him up.

I had put it in God's hands, and God worked it out. It took a huge load off of me—especially the worry about leaving Farrah. At least Sean knows I was going to show up for him until the producers made it impossible. I learned something very impor-tant from this experience, something I've seen over and over in the past: if I can just give a difficult situation to God, have faith, and let my mind be peaceful instead of being stressed out and anxious, it will all work out. It always does. And yet it seems I still have to be practically hit over the head with it before I finally get it. Sometimes fear can be so powerful that my faith temporarily goes out the window.

◈ *June 28, 2008*

It's starting to seem like we'll never get out of here. As of now, we're booked to leave on Tuesday, but Farrah was sick again today. I've never seen her so weak and frail. Every time she eats, she gets nauseated and throws up. Dr. Jacob says it's because her liver is still so swollen from the perfusion as well as the three surgeries before it. I feel like they're doing way too much to her body. I'm afraid they're going to kill her trying to cure her. I'm starting to think about getting her home on an ambulance plane and putting her into St. John's in L.A. I have faith in Dr. Jacob—and there's no one more brilliant in her approach to treating cancer—but she does really push the limits.

I went by Mimmo's for lunch and sat outside in the garden at his special table, tucked away under an arbor of green trees and surrounded by colorful summer flowers. As I sat looking out at the people dining under the azure blue umbrellas, the tables covered with crisp white linens, I had the most fabulous lunch: a salad of arugula and Pecorino, and homemade macaroni with turkey Bolognese.

When he came over to join me and have his lunch, Mimmo said he had to leave early because he had a pedicure appointment. I couldn't believe it! I said I'd never seen a man do so much to himself—pedicures, bronzing, bicycling, spinning, working out at the gym. But am I forgetting who I was married to? Rod, when I met him, wore leopard stretch pants and eye makeup (only onstage, thank God) and was very high maintenance. Then there's George, who has more shoes than Imelda Marcos and Ivana

Trump put together, and who takes longer to get ready to go out than I do.

Mimmo said it was very important to him to be well groomed, and also for any woman he's with to be the same. I was glad I wasn't wearing sandals. I haven't had a pedicure in six weeks. Somehow cancer, Farrah's and mine, has trumped manicures, pedicures, and getting roots done.

I told him I felt things were different between us and asked if he felt it, too. He said that when he came back after his last trip to Los Angeles, he missed me so much that it was very painful for him. He said he realized that there was no way we could see each other more than a few times a year and that he felt he had to pull back a little to "protect his heart."

It felt good to clear the air and talk about our feelings, but I don't think either of us knows where to go from here. Will we become just friends? I guess time will sort it out. We don't have any future that I can see. I'm not in love with him . . . or am I? I surely can't imagine myself married to him. It's kind of sad. It's been a lovely romance, but maybe it's time for it to end.


❧ *June 29, 2008*


Yet another crisis! Farrah's much better, thank God, and wants to leave on Tuesday, but now there are other issues with the kids.

Kimberly called and said she's really having a hard time and wants to come here. When it comes to the kids, I know Rod always thinks that I'm overprotective, and that they're grown and should be able to handle their own lives. That's true, to a large extent, but kids sometimes need some help and support from their parents, no matter what their age. She's just moved to another country, which alone is incredibly stressful, but she's also dealing with having bought an apartment and trying to decorate it while negotiating complicated work contracts. Not to mention that everyone is giving her different advice. She feels understandably overwhelmed and, on top of it, isn't feeling at all well physically. I'm worried about her. She wants to come here today, so I'm trying to arrange it. Now I'm leaving Tuesday, and I feel pulled again in different directions. I don't want to desert my daughter when she needs me, and yet I can't let Farrah travel on her own. Oh God, why is this happening *again*?

### June 30, 2008

I guess God doesn't want me to leave yet. Kim arrived last night around 10 P.M. I was so happy to see her. She begged me to stay longer, but Farrah was pretty intent on leaving Tuesday. She felt much better today, and she insisted on doing aquatics for quite a long time in the pool, which I thought was too much too soon, but of course she's very determined when she wants to do something. I'd really prefer leaving Wednesday or Thursday, so I could spend more time with Kimberly, but I don't know if Farrah will budge. My feeling is that we've been here five weeks, so what's two more days going to matter?

Unfortunately, the decision was taken out of my hands. Far-rah was sick again all night. Now Dr. Jacob says there's no way we can leave tomorrow. I'm sorry it's because she's not well, but I'm relieved at the same time. It's a lot to finalize—the bills, the tips, the packing, not to mention organizing all the medications we have to take home.

### July 1, 2008

Kim and I had a really nice dinner at Mimmo's. I was sur-prised at how nice she was to him, and he was so sweet to both of us. He'd bought me a bag of the white peaches he knows I love. When we got back to the clinic, Kim asked why I didn't go have a drink and "hang out" with Mimmo. I told her things were a little strained and complicated at the moment. We ended up sit-ting in my room, talking for a really long time. She said she thought Mimmo was great looking and very sweet and pointed out how much he tries to please me. "Mom, he even bought you those apricots and *I* didn't even know you liked them." White peaches, I told her, but never mind.

She asked me about her dad and me—how we met, why we broke up. She said he always told her the biggest problem was that I didn't like his friends. I admitted that was partly true and that I knew I was wrong. I'd realized after the fact that I regretted re-senting his friends and his soccer playing. I think I resented anything—his work included—that took him away from me and the kids. He had his part, too, like staying out all night with the boys in the band after a recording session. As it became a regular occurrence, I became angrier because it was so different from the way things had been in the beginning. We'd been so wrapped up in each other, so madly in love in the first couple of years of our relationship, and when it began to slowly change, I desperately tried to hold on to what it had been.

Now, of course, I know that's never possible. Relationships always evolve and change. But I didn't understand that at the time; neither of us did. We were just both immature and stubborn.

This conversation was the first time Kimberly and I had ever talked so intimately. I feel like we're starting to have a closer relationship, which is what I've prayed for, for a long time. I love my daughter so much. She can certainly be difficult, but she's getting more open and understanding, and I really want to try to make up for whatever I didn't or couldn't do when she was younger.

It's strange how things happen for the better when you least expect them. That a new relationship with my daughter should emerge in the midst of all this hell and chaos. I am learning so much about myself, about how if you open your heart, God heals it in wonderful ways. Had I not been here with Farrah, Kim and I never would have had this time together to talk and reconnect.

Maybe I'm also a changed person these days. A little sadder, yes, but a little wiser. A little more appreciative of what really matters in life. I feel like this experience of putting someone's needs before my own has spilled over into other areas of my life as well. Once you start to be a more giving person, it feels good, it feels right. People think that when you give, you deplete yourself. But I know now that it's the opposite; the more you give, the more you get in return.

### July 2, 2008

Well, we're finally leaving tomorrow. Farrah's much better today. I'm a little nervous about the flight home. I just hope she's not leaving too soon, like the time before, when she insisted on leaving five days after laser surgery on her liver. It was a horrendous trip home, and I don't ever want to go through that again, for her sake or mine.

Dr. Jacob said she's thrilled with the results of Farrah's treatment, that Farrah has made remarkable progress in these five weeks. She even went so far as to say that she considers Farrah in partial remission. This is unbelievable. Now, if things start to go more smoothly, and God forbid no more setbacks, she can go home and continue to get stronger.

### July 3, 2008

We're on the plane back to Los Angeles. Farrah's sleeping in the seat next to me. She could barely get herself together at the clinic to make it onto the plane—her usual packing chaos. Fortunately, I'd lied to her about the time (I don't know why I didn't try that sooner), and there wasn't horrible traffic, so we made the plane in good time. I knew in my heart that she should have waited a few more days, but she was hell-bent and determined to get home. I told her if she threw up all the way home that she wouldn't have to worry about dying, because I would kill her!

She was just starting to feel very nauseated and in a lot of pain, so I gave her the pain shot that Dr. Jacob had given me. It did the trick. Please, God, just let us get to L.A. without any problems, get through customs, get in the car, and get home. They'll have a wheelchair at the plane, and with luck there will be no paparazzi.

We arrived in Los Angeles without any incidents. Not even any paparazzi. We stopped at our favorite Starbucks by the airport and I got us chai teas, and then we dropped Farrah off and Benny took me to the house. I don't think I've ever been so happy to see my dogs.

### July 4, 2008

I celebrated the Fourth of July by doing absolutely nothing. I was so jet-lagged that all I wanted to do was to be home with the dogs and Fox News. Farrah and Ryan didn't go to the beach. The nurse that I had arranged for with Dr. Piro has been there helping her. I'm trying to unpack a little at a time and make some headway with the stacks of mail.

### July 6, 2008

Farrah said she was craving smothered chicken and black-eyed peas and it sounded so good that I decided to cook a southern meal like we had when we were growing up in Texas. I asked Sean and Ashley to come to dinner by themselves because I wanted to talk to them. I decided to tell them about the cancer episode before Rod told Sean, if he hadn't already. Rod knows because apparently Kimberly was in Harrods with him when she found out and she burst into tears.

Anyway, I feel like it was a wake-up call for all of us to be closer and to realize how important family is. I cooked the entire meal in two hours: smothered chicken, mashed potatoes, black-eyed peas, broccoli, cornbread, and peach cobbler—almost as good as Mama used to make.

After dinner, I took Ashley and Sean into my bedroom. Sean asked me if I was "dying or something." He said it sort of jokingly, but obviously his father had already opened his mouth. I prefaced it by saying that I was okay and didn't want to scare them, but after thinking a lot about it, I thought they should know. I said that I hoped we could all be closer and spend more time together as a family, and that it was important to love and support one another because you never know what's going to happen in life.

Ash was visibly shaken. Sean said his dad had already told him, which I figured. I'm glad we talked. I want to spend more time with my kids and I want them to be more supportive and loving with one another. Being with Farrah this past year and seeing all she's gone through has made me realize how much time I spend rushing through life. I know my kids do, too. Maybe we all do these days. But it's time for me to slow down and really appreciate the love I have in my life.

◈ *July 18, 2008*

I just meditated on an amazing page in *A Course in Miracles*. The title of the lesson is "I will be still an instant and go home." The part that stood out so clearly was about how there is this child inside each of us who is seeking comfort, but it won't be found in the outer world. We must go inside, be still, let the world recede from our minds, let valueless ideas spinning in our heads be quiet, and hear His voice. In that instant, we will be at home, our true home, "in perfect peace, beyond all words, untouched by fear and doubt, sublimely certain that we are home." I realized that this is what I've been searching for. I'm deeply exhausted and depleted—mentally, physically, emotionally—and I desperately wish I had someone to just put their arms around me and tell me everything will be okay.

Farrah and I were talking about that yesterday: a deep philosophical conversation. I said how nice it would be to have a man take care of me for a change. How a nice, boring, stable man suddenly looks so attractive to me at this point in my life. But maybe it doesn't ever come from a man? Or maybe, I told her, it can only come from a higher source. From going inside and connecting with that sense of peace and joy and power inside of us.

All I know is that I felt this deep, deep sense of letting go. I felt this golden light wash over me, and I felt a sense of comfort and peace that I've never felt before. I felt as if someone were actually cradling me and telling me I'm safe. I felt such a sense of well-being. I've searched for this feeling in everything: men, drugs, spiritual pursuits. I'd go anywhere to try to get it, even if only momentarily, and I just felt it so deeply, with such an intensity.

Will it last? I don't know. But I know I feel like my tank has been filled. I feel like I can go to London, be there for Kimberly, do whatever I need to do to take care of my own life, without feeling so deeply, desperately depleted. Without feeling like I'm running on empty.

I have to remember that this is the place I must go; that it's always available to me. I don't need to continue looking for it in all the wrong places.

### August 29, 2008

I got up at six thirty this morning to come out to the City of Hope with Farrah and Ryan. She's starting a new clinical trial treatment today with Dr. Forman. It's called the IT-101 and everyone feels very hopeful and optimistic about it. The actual trial itself was completed a couple of years ago by about twenty people, but no results have been released yet because it's not FDA approved and I guess they have to wait a certain amount of time. The doctor had to get special permission to do it now with her. She's spent the last six weeks waiting to get cleared for this trial, and during this time she hasn't been able to take any of her anticancer medications from Germany. Apparently they might interfere with this new treatment.

It's 4:30 P.M. and I've come downstairs to get some tea and some fresh air. Farrah is having the chemo infusion now, which takes six hours altogether, so we probably won't be leaving here until seven or eight. I'm exhausted, but I'm glad I came. I've been filming most of the day and I think I got some great footage. This film is probably going to be difficult for people to watch at times. Like today, when it took almost an hour for the nurse to get the needle into one of Farrah's veins because they're all so shot from chemo and IVs during the last two years. It was excruciatingly painful for her and so hard to watch her go through it. She's so brave.

### ❖ September 26, 2008

Yesterday I picked Farrah up at 8 A.M. to drive to the City of Hope for her third treatment of chemo in this trial. It was a long, grueling day for her. Nothing seemed to go smoothly. As usual, they couldn't find a vein for the IV line. After numerous tries by two different nurses, they were finally successful, but then the doctor had to wait for her blood results before he could write up the order for the chemo. We didn't leave there until almost ten o'clock at night. I don't know how she gets through it. I was completely exhausted.

I think I don't allow myself to fully accept that she's truly fighting for her life, and if this trial doesn't work, there may not be a next step. I can't conceive of it; it doesn't seem possible. She looks so good—you would hardly know she was ill. She's just the same Farrah I've always known; we're two girlfriends talking about our lives, our children, our clothes. Yet now a lot of our conversation revolves around cancer. She still maintains her sense of humor, though. Today she was joking about filling in the order forms to renew her magazine subscriptions. She said, "You have to check one year, two years, or three years. Hmm. I always wonder which one I should put." Again, she finds the humor in almost every situation.

As for me, it's hard for me to believe all this is real. We both said we feel like Alice in Wonderland. Nothing is real and we're walking through a dream. I wish we would wake up and it would all be gone.

P.S. I have my own medical update. My Pap test came back from UCLA and it's not normal again. I'm still trying to understand Dr. Rapkin's very complicated explanation. I have to do a test every four months, and if it goes to the next stage, then I have to have another biopsy. Then, if it turns into cancer, a radical hysterectomy! I can't quite believe all this is happening again. Of course she said that in only 10 percent of women does it actually turn into cancer. God, I feel like I'm living with a possible time bomb inside me. Maybe I'm being overly dramatic, but just thinking about it terrifies me. So I guess I won't think about it. I can't do anything about it now anyway.

*September 27, 2008*

I was finishing baking my cake to take to the movie tonight at Carole and Bob's when Farrah called. She could barely speak. She's been throwing up nonstop since six this morning. I said I'd come right over and take her to the hospital, but as usual she resisted.

"Okay, but I'm going to call Dr. Piro," I said. When I reached Dr. Piro, I told him she sounded terrible and asked if he would call her right away and then call me back. He said that he told Farrah to dissolve two Ativan under her tongue and that would relax her, put her to sleep, and hopefully stop the vomiting. I tried to reach her afterward, but there was no answer, so I assumed she was already sleeping.

I left for Carole and Bob's house, but I was worried because I still hadn't heard from Farrah. I was relieved to see Dr. Piro there, who was a guest for the movie as well. We tried to call her together, but once again there was no answer.

"She's probably just sleeping," he said, and I agreed with him. But I still hadn't heard from her when I went to bed later. I couldn't sleep; I kept tossing and turning. I was worried out of my mind. I thought about going over there, but the doorman probably wouldn't have let me up without calling and she wasn't answering the phone. Maybe I was just being silly. She was probably sleeping soundly. It's just that I can't get the memories of my mother out of my head. Many years ago, when I was married to George, I had kept calling and calling her and she didn't answer. I just assumed she'd turned off her phone as she usually did when she wanted to sleep and didn't want to be bothered. But that wasn't the case this time. She died of an overdose of drugs, and I wasn't there to save her.

Finally, I fell into a fitful sleep, making sure I'd left the phone right next to my bed.

### ❖ *September 28, 2008*

Farrah finally called this morning. She had been up and down all night throwing up. She was still weak, but finally the vomiting had stopped. I told her she can't stay in that apartment alone like this. Someone has to be there with her. She's so independent and doesn't think she needs it, but I see it differently.

### ❖ *September 30, 2008*

I took Ashley to Il Sole for his birthday. He brought three of his friends and it was a really lovely, quiet evening. It's wonderful to see him sober and looking so good and seemingly in a good place. I guess I'll always worry about him after all the years when he was using. I noticed he had started smoking again, and that scares me, of course.

### ❖ *October 5, 2008*

Farrah called tonight. I've never heard her sound so low and so hopeless. She said that sometimes she felt like she couldn't go on, that she didn't feel like fighting anymore. It was all too much. I can't blame her. How much can one person take? Two years of painful treatments, life-altering surgeries, and now going through these problems with her son. She told me that she's afraid Red-

This was taken at a party at my house back in 1984.
Farrah and I are with my daughter Kimberly and my son Sean.

Here we are at a dinner party I threw at my house for Elton John in 1987.
When Elton arrived he turned to me and asked, "Where's the piano?" to
which I replied that I didn't have one. The next morning, a delivery truck
arrived in my driveway with, what else, a baby grand from Elton.
*Front row (left to right):* Wendy Stark, Suzanne de Passe,
me, Farrah, and Tina Sinatra.
*Back row (left to right):* Bob Halley,
David Niven Jr., Ryan O'Neal, and Elton John.

This is from New Year's Eve 1986, during the last bash
at the house I shared with Rod. I was moving out two days later,
so I was ready to celebrate a new beginning with my friends.

A quiet dinner out in Malibu with good friends in 1987.
*From left to right:* me, Ryan, Farrah, and Michael Black.

Farrah snuggling up to Ryan at my birthday party in 1989.

Birthdays were always a big deal for us, and we made sure to celebrate the milestones each year. This photo was taken at Farrah's birthday in 1988 as she tried on one of her presents.

At the *Mirabella* magazine party, June 1989.
*From left to right:* Jerry and Linda Bruckheimer,
Ryan, Farrah, me, and Tina Sinatra.

Alan Carr, Tina Sinatra, Ryan, and Farrah
at the home of Tina's father, Frank Sinatra.

Me, a young Kimberly, and Farrah. Growing up, my
daughter always admired Farrah's style.

For my birthday in 1989, Suzanne de Passe threw me a party at her house.
The theme was country-western, and she served Texas soul food and
hired a band to play country tunes.
*From left to right:* me, Suzanne de Passe, Farrah, and Tina Sinatra.

Farrah truly
looks overjoyed
here at her
birthday in 1991.

Ryan and Farrah have
always been the golden
couple to me.

For my birthday in 1991, Alan Carr threw me a dinner party at the Four Seasons in Los Angeles. Here I am pictured with the host *(far right)*, Farrah, and Barry Diller *(second from the left)*.

A snapshot of just the girls at my birthday in 1991.
*From left to right:* Dyan Cannon, me, Tina Sinatra, and Farrah.

Farrah with my daughter Kimberly.

Farrah and Ryan ringing in the holidays at my home in 1992.

Laurie Lynn Stark, a friend of ours who owns the store Chrome Hearts, took photos with this big old-fashioned Polaroid. Farrah and I stopped by the showroom and didn't expect to be photographed — I didn't have a stitch of makeup on. But I think it looks like we both have attitude.

Almost a week after I found out about Farrah's diagnosis, Tina Sinatra and I went over to Farrah's house to see her for the first time. Tina brought Farrah this humongous bear. Despite the chemo, our friend looked radiant and determined to fight.

Mimmo asked us to pose with him in this photo so he could hang it in his restaurant.

It was Christmas 2007 and Farrah and I whipped up our traditional holiday pies — pecan and coconut meringue.

We spent New Year's Eve 2007 at Tina Sinatra's. We had dinner, watched a movie in our pj's, tuned in to the ball dropping in Times Square at midnight, and celebrated with some champagne.

Farrah with Kimberly and me during Christmas 2007.

Farrah with her son Redmond and my daughter Kimberly
at the Leonardis Clinic in June 2007.

In March 2008, Farrah and I escaped to Mexico shortly after her fourth trip to Germany when they declared her tumor free. It was the last time I remember Farrah really feeling good for a prolonged period of time.

As difficult as it was sometimes to be in Germany, the clinic was in such a beautiful part of Bavaria that it made things a little easier.

Keeping the faith in May 2008. Farrah was back in the hospital just before surgery with Dr. Kiehling. She's holding her rosaries, as she always did before any surgery or procedure. It was her ritual to say a quick prayer and kiss them.

Me, Dr. Jacob, Farrah, and Ryan enjoying dinner on our first trip to Germany.

Here we are at a makeshift slumber party in February 2008.
This very sweet girl, Francoise Shirley, who had a company called
Sleepyheads, asked if we could send her a picture of us in the pj's.
We loved these flannel pj's, so we put Farrah's pink boa around
our necks and climbed into her bed at the clinic to pose.

mond may go to prison. I know how she feels; I've been there, too. It's something we talk about often: our kids. I told her that Sean just went back into rehab and how worried I've been about him. At least now, I told her, I can breathe a little easier, knowing he's safe, even if it's just for thirty days.

We talked for a long time, and when we hung up she was in better spirits. I told her it's only normal to feel hopeless and depressed with all she's going through. I don't know how she's doing it. I tell her again and again that she doesn't realize how courageous she is, that she's the bravest person I've ever known.

Her scan is this week, and we'll know if the tumors are smaller, larger, or the same. She's scared. I keep telling her it's going to be okay, but truthfully, I'm scared, too. God, we just need a miracle. Please let there be good news. I don't know how much more of this she can take. Thank you, God. Amen.

❖ *October 9, 2008*

This is the big day. I'm sitting here in the waiting room at Dr. Piro's clinic while Farrah waits for the radioactive material they've just injected her with to take effect. Then they will do the CT and PET scans. We were just laughing and talking . . . like we would on any normal day, about clothes, where we would eat afterward, going by to look at Jaguars if we had time. And yet after these scans are done, we'll know the results, and her life could be radically changed—yet again. If the tumors haven't responded to the trial at City of Hope and have grown larger or multiplied, I can't even imagine what the next step will be. But I'm not going there now. I feel in my heart it's going to be good news. But I've been wrong before, time and time again. So I'm frightened.

**Later**

It wasn't exactly good news. Dr. Piro called us into the scan room and showed us on the screens where the active tumors were. We were both pretty shocked to hear that not only have the ones in the liver grown larger and multiplied but the primary one has returned and there appears to be activity in a lymph gland as well. Farrah didn't cry. She asked questions and listened thoughtfully to the answers, but she was so disappointed. This was so not what we had expected. Dr. Piro went on to say that the growth might have occurred during the five or six weeks while she was waiting for Dr. Forman to get the approval to start the trial. He called Dr. Forman, who said that he would like to do three more treatments and then recheck the tumors in six weeks. He feels he needs more time for the drugs to work (if they're going to was the part left unsaid).

I think we both grasped onto the hope that the drug will kick in and the next scan will show an improvement. We were both quiet when we got into the car. Finally, I just said, "I'm so sorry." She got teary, but stayed amazingly strong and brave. She seems so fragile right now, my heart just breaks for her. I searched for something to say that would cheer her up, some thread of optimism. I reminded her that the man who was in the documentary about this chemo trial had been given two weeks to live and this drug saved him and he was still alive and thriving some years later.

We had planned to possibly go look at Jaguars today because her car lease was up and she needed to find another one right away. I figured it was out of the question now, but she said, out of the blue, "Let's go look at those Jags." So we put it all behind us and went off to the Jag showroom. Soon we were oohing and aahing over the beautiful new cars and it was as if we were just girlfriends on a shopping trip again. In the end, the man wasn't able to give her a very good deal, so we went straight to Mercedes, where she found a car she loved.

When she had to make the decision about the number of years she wanted to lease it, she looked at me and smiled wryly. "This is where I always have trouble . . ."

*Even in the middle of everything, we still had girls' night in.*

*It was right after New Year's, January 2, 2009. Farrah, Tina, Wendy Stark, and I all went over to Tina's new house so that Farrah could see it. I was so glad she was getting out of the house for a fun evening. She needed it; we all did.*

*Tina's house was so warm and Christmasy. We posed in front of the twinkling Christmas tree, which Tina always keeps up long after Christmas. Wendy brought a pound of decadent caviar, and we ate it on baked potatoes that Tina made. Farrah looked so good, so vibrant. Amazing, in fact, considering all she'd been through. We toasted to her health with champagne.*

*After a while, Farrah started to feel weak and had to lie down. Suddenly it was like we were back in reality, the past two years catching up with us in an instant. She was having these weird symptoms—one leg was swollen twice the size of the other one—and we were hoping for answers on Monday when she had a scan.*

*Just for this brief moment, this girls' get-together, we were happy and not thinking of what tomorrow or Monday might hold. We were not worrying about Farrah or the doctors or cancer. We were simply in the here and now with the happiness and hope of a bright new year—a group of friends who'd been through it all.*

# LOOKING FOR A MIRACLE

❖ *October 21, 2008*

I had to find all of Sean's test results tonight so I could take it to the rehab center tomorrow. He came to me and said he'd relapsed and that he would like to go back into treatment. I'm so proud of him for making that decision on his own. I feel that this experience is going to help him grow up and become a responsible young man. I really believe in him; I always have.

❖ *November 4, 2008*

What a horrible, horrible day—for so many reasons. I woke up feeling terrible—cramps in my stomach, weak, dizzy. I ran out to vote and stopped by to check on Farrah. There has been a nurse at the house since yesterday morning because she started throwing up again and couldn't stop. I was alarmed to see how frail she was.

I called Dr. Piro and he wanted me to bring her straight to the hospital. She could barely make it into my car, and when she got there, I had to lay her down in the backseat. Of course then

I had to maneuver my way through bumper-to-bumper traffic all the way to the hospital. The whole time I could hear her moaning, and I kept trying to catch a glimpse of her in the rear-view mirror. By the time we finally got there, the hospital direc-tor was waiting outside with a wheelchair, and he promptly took her to a room.

For the first time, I fear that this could be one of those set-backs that Dr. Jacob talked about and that she might not come out of it. I talked to Dr. Piro at length and we both agree that he's got to keep her there and do whatever tests are necessary to find out what's causing the vomiting and the bleeding. He even mentioned the possibility of exploratory surgery. Right now everything looks dark and hopeless. Where is my faith, God? Help me get it back.

### November 5, 2008

I'm waiting for Dr. Piro to call me back about Farrah. I just spoke to her in the hospital and she sounds much better, more like her old self. She was giving some nurse hell because she couldn't get a grilled cheese sandwich.

"I can hear you're better," I said to her, "because you're mean as a snake." She always gets that way on pain medication.

### November 7, 2008

I just got home from the hospital. I want to cry, but it's like the tears are all blocked up inside me. I feel like I'm a robot going through the motions, or one of the pod people from *Invasion of the Body Snatchers*.

When I spoke to Farrah this morning she sounded drugged and confused. She thought she was having an MRI but wasn't sure. I spoke to Dr. Piro and he said she was going to have a colonoscopy and biopsy. He'd know more about what was going on when he got the results later. I called Farrah back, explained what was going on, and told her I'd come to see her afterward.

"Is there anything I can bring you?" I asked.

"Anything you're baking," she replied.

"I'm baking a cake for the movie at Carole and Bob's tonight. I'll bring you a slice."

Around four thirty I called Dr. Piro and he was in Farrah's room talking to her. Somehow I knew by the tone of his voice that it wasn't a good conversation. I said to tell her I'd be over there shortly. I was on the way to the hospital, nerves on edge, when he called me back and confirmed my fears: the original tumor has gotten larger and has to be removed as soon as possible. The treatment at City of Hope is obviously not working. He mentioned CyberKnife surgery and that he was looking into various options.

"She's pretty upset about it," he added. "Try to stay positive when you see her."

I walked into the room while she was trying to eat a little of the bland dinner on her hospital tray. She looked at me and started to cry.

"The IT-101's not working," she said.

That said it all. During the four months since we came back from the clinic, the tumors have not only increased in size but they've spread. I told her not to lose hope, that Dr. Piro felt there were a number of options. The nurse came in to give her more pain medication, and soon Farrah was barely coherent. But she was determined to eat some of my homemade cake, so she dove into a piece.

While she was in the middle of eating it, she drifted off to sleep. As I began to gently lift the container from her chest, she suddenly grabbed it with both hands.

"You're not taking that anywhere," she said, and we both laughed.

She drifted in and out of sleep from the heavy sedation. Then, out of the blue, she said, "I'm going to miss you so much." It was all I could do not to cry.

"You won't miss me because you're not going anywhere." Part of me wants to still believe that, but it's getting harder every day.

At one point, I thought she'd gone to sleep, so I started to tip-toe out the door. Just as I was sneaking out she called my name. She clearly didn't want me to go, so I sat down again by her bedside. I said nothing; there was nothing to say. We just hugged each other for a long time, and I finally left as she drifted off to sleep.

I came home and went through the motions of getting ready for bed. For the first time in probably five years, I didn't turn on Fox News the minute I walked in the house. I just needed the silence. I talked to Dr. Piro again tonight and asked point-blank, "She's not going to make it, is she?"

"She'll pull through this now, but if you're asking me if she's going to beat it, the answer is no," he replied.

I guess I've known it for some time now. From Dr. Vogl, when we spoke in Frankfurt, and certainly from the last scan, but now it seems more imminent.

I spoke to Ryan from my cell phone in the hallway outside her room. I could feel his sadness through the phone.

"It's ironic, isn't it?" he said. "I feel like I've done this movie before, but Ali MacGraw is still alive." He meant *Love Story*, of course.

I can't allow myself to think about losing this battle, about losing her.

❖ *November 8, 2008*

I talked to Farrah this morning and she told me she'd fallen down in the night and hurt herself. She'd been throwing up again as well. I went to see her at the hospital around six. She was sleeping soundly and I didn't want to wake her. I sat in the dark room for almost an hour, looking at my frail yet still beautiful friend, hooked up to monitors and IVs. It breaks my heart. I know I keep saying that, but I don't know how else to describe the way I feel. It's as if there's a big, gaping hole in my chest and it aches something fierce. It's as if I'm grieving—but she's not gone yet. I have to keep reminding myself of that. Farrah is full of surprises.

One time, when we were in Germany and Kim was there, Farrah admired her beautiful leopard-print pony-skin Yves Saint Laurent handbag. We both thought the bag was exquisite, and when we got home, Farrah was still thinking about it.

"You should buy one," I told her. "I can't afford it, but you can. You should get one."

So she did, and she just loved it. Farrah is by no means an extravagant person. She still has her Texas values like me: "Don't throw your money away." But it was such a happy splurge, and she deserved it after all she's been through. Then, after the next trip home from Germany, I was dropping her off at her home, and her assistant came downstairs with a huge box. In it was the YSL bag—the exact one Farrah had bought for herself. She wanted to thank me for what I had done for her. I was so touched, so surprised, and whenever I carry it, I think of Farrah.

◈ *November 9, 2008*

I just talked to Dr. Piro for a long time. He'd just been in to see Farrah and she's doing better today. The situation with the tumor is not good, however. He's looking into the possibility of doing CyberKnife surgery, which is using a radiation technique to kill the tumor, but that may not be possible because of all the radiation she had at UCLA in the beginning. She was told, after the fact (of course), that she could never have radiation again in that area. So we won't know until tomorrow. If that's not an option, he has to investigate what all the others might be, as far as chemotherapy, to shrink the tumor.

◈ *November 10, 2008*

I called the Christian Science Reading Room to get the name of a practitioner for Farrah. Marianne Williamson had suggested

I get her the books and tapes, so I went over there several days ago to pick them up, and I started looking through one of the little pamphlets. I was reading about some of the healing miracles people have had and decided to call one of their practitioners. I spoke to a very nice lady who agreed to come to the hospital and see Farrah tomorrow. Meanwhile she would start prayer work.

◆ *November 11, 2008*

I told Ryan I'd meet him at the hospital around 1 P.M. and that hopefully we'd be able to talk to Dr. Piro together. Farrah was doing much better today. The difference from yesterday was astounding. She was on very little pain medication and was much like her old self. Dr. Piro came in and told us what the options were and what he thought was the best way to proceed. It boils down to not having surgery but instead using chemo to try to shrink the primary tumor as well as the ones in the liver. He said he'd spoken to Dr. Vogl in Frankfurt and was waiting to hear from Dr. Jacob. I had spoken to them both earlier, and they would prefer she come back to Germany, but Dr. Piro feels that she's too weak to make that trip now. I hope this chemo treatment goes well and she gets stronger again, so we can go back to Germany. It seems like the only place she's had any success with treatment.

After Ryan left, I told Farrah about the Christian Science practitioner and that the woman had been praying for her since last night. "That's amazing," she said, "because I started feeling so much better around midnight."

I told Farrah that the practitioner would come to the hospital, and she very much wanted her to. I called the woman and she said she'd be there in a couple of hours. When she arrived, it was quite a fascinating experience. Her name was Diane, and she was a lovely woman, probably in her fifties, who talked to us about Mary Baker Eddy, the founder of the church. She spoke about the principles of Christian Science, which basically says that we are spiritual beings, not mortal, and therefore disease, pain, suffering, and death are all false ideas, and not the truth about us.

"You have to see Farrah as God's perfect child, free of disease and suffering," she instructed me. She didn't actually pray with us—she does that part of it in her meditation at home. She said that I could read the textbook to Farrah and that I should especially say the Lord's Prayer, that it was a very powerful healing prayer.

After she had gone, I stayed for a few minutes and read Psalm 23 out loud: "The Lord is my shepherd . . ." Farrah seemed very calm and at peace. I really think there's something to this Christian Science business. I headed for home feeling more positive than I have in a long time.

*November 13, 2008*

Farrah had the new chemo late last night and it went very well. Fortunately, she didn't get sick from it. At the hospital, I called Diane, the Christian Science practitioner, and she spoke to Farrah on the speakerphone. I read a little out loud from the book before I left. Maybe this is the miracle we've been asking for. Things seem to be going so much better since this lady has been praying for Farrah. She's leaving the hospital this morning to go back home.

## November 15, 2008

Farrah and I may be going back to Germany. We both spoke to Dr. Jacob at length yesterday and she has some ideas that she feels certain could help Farrah. We'd have to leave on the first of December and be gone three weeks. That means getting home just before Christmas. I'm not sure how I feel about it, but if we have to go, we'll just go. If this chemo that she just had is working, maybe we could go after Christmas instead. I'd prefer that, but maybe Farrah shouldn't take the chance. It's so hard to know what's right.

## November 28, 2008

It's the day after Thanksgiving and I'm exhausted from cooking for two days. Farrah was feeling well enough to come over two nights in a row and make pies with me. This new chemo appears to be working, which means we have even more to be thankful for. We won't go to Germany until after the first of January. God, I'm relieved not to have to miss the holidays at home.

She was able to come for dinner last night. I can't help wondering how many more Thanksgivings and Christmases she has left. I hate that I even have that thought, but I guess it's only natural for it to cross my mind. She talks about it herself. She doesn't know how much time she has . . . a year, two, maybe five? I know there can be a miracle, but the chances seem to be getting more remote with every new scan.

## December 4, 2008

This healer from the Philippines, Father Fernando Suarez, came to see Farrah today. He was a small, dark-skinned man with a powerful presence. A friend of ours had called to tell me about him, and I set up an appointment for him to come see her. Apparently people have had amazing healing experiences from just seeing him one time. He prayed for her with his hands on her body and gave her two bracelets to wear and a prayer to say every day. Afterward he came over to me. The minute he touched my body I started to cry. He pointed to my chest and said I had a lingering virus that was causing me to be susceptible to other viruses that come along. Exactly what I've been experiencing. He prayed and gave me the same bracelets to wear and blessed some water for both of us to drink.

Afterward we both felt drugged. I did a few errands and then went home feeling just wiped out. I got into my flannel pajamas and crawled into bed and stayed there the rest of the evening. Farrah and I talked later and she felt the same. Maybe it's our bodies healing. God, I hope so.

## ❖ December 25, 2008

It's Christmas night and everyone has eaten and gone on their way. I should feel happy at having spent a lovely night with my children and my friends, but I'm feeling unbearably sad. Farrah looked so frail tonight. Every day she has horrible side effects from this last round of chemo, and we don't even know for sure if it's working.

Last night she came over to make pies. I know she could barely make it, but she loves doing it and pushes herself beyond her limits to get here. I don't know if I'm starting to sense that the cancer is getting the best of her or if it's just fear, but I think I know deep down in my heart that it's a matter of time now. When she hugged me tonight and said she loved me, I could almost feel every bone in her body through her skin. Please, God, let her be around a lot longer. I need her. She knows I'm useless with the damn crusts and can't do them without her.

I just spoke to Marianne and she said a prayer for Farrah. I feel better. Sad still, but better. I called Ash and Sean to tell them I love them. I wish Kim had been here. She's called a couple of times sounding sad and lonely. She told her dad she'd never spent Christmas without her mom and he said she lived in London now. It always astounds me that he can sometimes be so lacking in compassion.

## December 26, 2008

Farrah called earlier and was on her way to the emergency room. Her right leg has swollen to twice the size of the other one, and Dr. Piro is concerned that it could be a blood clot. She was in tears and didn't want to have to go into the hospital again. I told her I would meet her there, but she said she'd call as soon as they did the ultrasound.

She just called and it's not a blood clot but they're not sure what it is. The doctor thinks maybe the lymph system isn't draining on her right side because the tumor is blocking it. Good God, doesn't she ever get a break? Dr. Piro was so sure the chemo was working; we thought the tumors must be shrinking. How can this be? I don't like the sound of this at all. They didn't make her stay in the hospital, though, and she said she'll call me as soon as she gets home.

## December 28, 2008

Farrah and I both spoke to Dr. Jacob today. She thinks Farrah should have a scan right away to see if the chemo has been working and the tumors are smaller. She's concerned about the swelling and that the tumors could have grown and therefore be causing the blockage in lymphatic drainage. She thinks we should come to Germany within the next two weeks. Farrah feels more comfortable being there in the clinic, and frankly, so do I.

The idea of leaving again makes me anxious, but if it's what needs to be done, I'll do it. After seeing that movie *Marley & Me* the other night, about the dog dying, I can't bear the thought of leaving my dog Lolita. She'll be nine in April, and although she still seems like a young dog, I know she can have only a few good years left. I've never felt this way about a dog—I've never been much of a dog person—but there's some special connection between us. We love each other so much. I can just lie down next to her and look at her sometimes. Then she gets annoyed and moves away. I can't believe I could be so obsessed with a dog. I remember when it used to be men!

## January 1, 2009

It's 2:30 A.M., the beginning of the new year! I went over to Farrah's to spend it with her and Ryan, and I'm so glad I did. She was feeling and looking so much better. It was really a sweet, lovely evening. We had some smoked salmon, made Bellinis, and watched Clint Eastwood's *Gran Torino*. We tuned in to see the ball drop at midnight and raised our glasses in a toast to good health—especially Farrah's. Then we made two piecrusts for tomorrow, and by that time it was almost two.

She has a scan on Monday and we'll know where everything stands then. I feel like it's going to be much better, but I've felt that way the last few times, and I've been wrong. I hope I'm not wrong again.

## January 5, 2009

I'm sitting in the waiting room at Dr. Piro's office, where Farrah will be having her scan in a few minutes. She's in an isolated room now, with the radioisotope substance in her veins, and they'll do the scan after forty-five minutes. She can't move or talk or read, and no one can be in the room with her because of the radioactive material in her veins.

She's feeling very hopeful, but I'm almost afraid to get too positive. Every time we have, we've gotten bad news, it seems. So I'm not going to jinx us. We'll know within the next two hours.

**Later**

I think Farrah and I were both holding our breath when Dr. Piro walked into the room after the scan. I know I was. He said, "Well, it's a good-news day!" He told us that the tumors are all shrinking; that this chemo is working. She was ecstatic. We all were. Dr. Piro was beaming as Farrah hugged him. It's the first time in so long that we've gotten good news, especially from the scans here.

We went to tea at the Peninsula to celebrate. Farrah called her dad, Ryan, and Redmond. We called Tina and Carole. We were all so happy. I told her I didn't think it was all the chemo, by any means. I think the spiritual work she's been doing with Marianne, Father Sanchez, and Diane, the Christian Science practitioner, is playing a big part. It's as if the energy has shifted.

*January 14, 2009*

Today the news is not so good: I got a call from the hospital that Farrah was being admitted. Just when things were looking up, she started vomiting nonstop at one o'clock this morning. It was obviously from the chemo she had yesterday. Marianne Williamson and I were supposed to have dinner, but we went down to see Farrah first. She was just lying there under all the covers, so still, so quiet, with IVs dripping into her arms. She looked pale, fragile, and helpless. She could barely speak. We just sat on the bed in the dark and Marianne prayed for her. The nurse came in and gave her some medication to put her out for the night. When she gets into one of these throwing-up jags, the only way to stop it is to put her to sleep. We crept quietly out when her eyes started to close.

We had dinner at Toscano, an Italian restaurant in Brentwood, where I used to live. The pasta wasn't quite as good as I remembered it. The kids and I lived in the Brentwood house for twelve years. I can't believe the time passed so quickly. Sometimes I wish I could go back in time and live it all over again. And be more present, and appreciate what I had more, appreciate my children more. Cherish every minute instead of always being so busy, busy, busy. Just another of the many, many regrets I have in my life. Things I wish I'd done differently.

It was bittersweet being back in Brentwood. I felt slightly sad and disconnected. Life is passing too quickly. Like a meteor flashing through the sky. I feel like I can't hold on to anything, especially Farrah. It gives me that old familiar feeling of being adrift in a sea with no anchor. Just lost at sea.

### ❦ January 31, 2009

Carole had an early birthday dinner for Farrah Saturday night. Jaclyn Smith and her husband, Brad, Kate Jackson, Jose, Carole, Bob, Tina, me, Dr. Piro and his wife, Judy, and Farrah and Ryan, of course. Farrah wanted a chocolate cake with white icing, so I volunteered to make it. It took me all day. The first one flopped. Gas was leaking out of my stove, so I had to call the gas company. Then I baked another one, even though the repair guy said not to use the stove. Geri Lugo, my manager and also a phenomenal baker, came over and decorated it, since I'm as useless at decorating cakes as I am at making piecrusts. They always taste incredibly good but are not so pretty. She made beautiful chocolate roses with a pastry tube. It fell over in my car on the way there, but I managed to salvage it.

Farrah is so depleted. This chemo is really wrecking her. She's been so sick all week. She was in the hospital for one night and has had nurses at home much of the rest of the time. I don't know how much more her body can take, although Dr. Piro says she's in much better shape than she was two months ago, when she was in the hospital so ill from the bleeding. He says that the chemo is shrinking the tumors, and that these symptoms are all from the chemo. She has no quality of life, but I guess that's the way it is when people are having such heavy doses of chemo.

The terrible part, besides the pain, is the indignities she has to go through. Losing her hair, constant vomiting, being so horribly weak and exhausted all the time. She made it through dinner and opening the presents, but had to leave about an hour into the movie. She wasn't feeling well at all. Where is this miracle that we need? It's time, God. She's suffered enough.

I wonder if we'll go back to Germany. I don't even know if she could travel at this point.

◈ *February 1, 2009*

Mimmo called today; he still does periodically. He said he had a dream about me last night, a very sexy dream. He said he misses me. I'm not sure how I feel anymore, but I do miss him—or at least I miss what we had in the beginning. And that's probably not going to come back. I asked him if he's been seeing anyone and he said (in Italian), "Yes, I've been dating a German girl some."

"Is it serious?" I asked half teasingly.

"No, no," he replied quickly. "I really don't know yet."

After we hung up, I thought to myself with a little pang, Hmm . . . he found someone awfully quickly.

◈ *February 9, 2009*

Boy, a lot has happened in a short space of time. Farrah had another scan and it wasn't good. The tumors have grown again and there is more cell activity. Dr. Jacob came into town and we met with her and Dr. Piro on Saturday. They both agree that Farrah has to go back to Germany for local treatment with Dr. Vogl. She can't have any more systemic chemo because her platelets are too low, so there really is no other option. Something has to be done right away to stop the tumors from continuing to grow. I hope she can make this trip. She is so weak she can barely walk into her kitchen, much less get on a plane and fly for twelve hours.

But she has no choice but to go, and I have no choice but to go with her.

*February 15, 2009*

We didn't leave today. Farrah got a bad infection in her arm from an IV site and has to be on intravenous antibiotics for a few days. The plan now is to leave on Wednesday, if all goes well.

*A beautiful mind.*

*This photo was taken on one of our last trips to Germany, while we were shooting footage for the documentary. I like that Farrah—despite all she was going through—looks so beautiful, so vibrant in this picture. She seems happy and even refreshed. You'd never know what horrors she has been through. There is not a hint of them written on her sweet, smiling face. I marvel at her resilience.*

*A number of years ago, I took Farrah to meet spiritual guru Deepak Chopra. I convinced her to go with me for a week to his healing center in Del Mar. Farrah, being Catholic, had always been fairly religious but was not very familiar with the spiritual path that I had been pursuing. Previously, I had tried to teach her how to meditate by choosing a calming word or mantra and going into a peaceful place inside yourself.*

*When she met Deepak, he asked her, "Farrah, do you know how to meditate?" She replied, "Oh, yes! I do it quite often. Mostly in the car when I'm driving." I think Deepak was probably speechless for the first time in his life.*

*Classic Farrah. Not even Deepak Chopra could change her. We laughed about her unique method of meditating for years.*

# BACK TO GERMANY

❖ *February 20, 2009*

Farrah and I finally made it. We got on Lufthansa yesterday (just barely, as usual) and arrived in Frankfurt at ten thirty this morning. We went by the hotel, dropped the bags, and went straight to Dr. Vogl at the hospital. He did the MRI first and the chemo embolization right afterward. When I got him alone to question him about how it went and what he thought, he wasn't very positive at all.

"It's a disaster," he said. "The primary tumor has grown very large and there is a tumor in her lymph that is blocking the drainage, which is why her left leg is swollen twice the size. I put ninety percent of the chemo into the primary area and the other ten percent into the liver." I asked why only 10 percent in the liver, and he said, "The primary had to be the priority today."

"How is the liver?" I asked.

"Not good." He shook his head. "There are maybe forty tumors now."

I thought maybe I'd heard wrong. "Forty?!" I asked, hoping he'd said fourteen and it was just the accent.

"Spend all the time you can with her," he said solemnly.

"What are you saying? How long do you think she has?" By now I was completely numb with shock.

"I don't know," he said. And then, "She could die any day."

I called Dr. Jacob afterward and asked if she'd spoken to Dr. Vogl. I told her what he'd told me and she said she knew. I asked her if I should call Ryan and get him to come over.

"Not yet," she said. "It would only complicate the situation right now. Let me do these tests and see how everything looks in a few days. If, or when, you need to, you can call him."

I can't say anything yet, not even to Ryan? It doesn't seem right. I feel like he should know, but I don't want to panic him prematurely.

I can't believe I could be losing my best friend. What am I saying? I *am* losing her. It's a matter of time. Though tonight, she sure didn't seem near death. She was disappointed that the news wasn't better, and she didn't even know the full extent of it. I look at her now and she doesn't look like Farrah. What is happening to my friend before my eyes? I want to make it all stop and go away and I can't.

❖ *February 22, 2009*

It's 2:30 A.M. I went to sleep around ten last night. I couldn't keep my eyes open, but sure enough, four hours later I'm wide awake. I just took one and a half Ativan, hoping that'll do the trick. The last thing I want is to be awake in the middle of the night with nothing to do but think. Earlier this evening, Farrah asked Eileen, the nurse who was with us in Frankfurt, what had happened to Jonathan, the nice Englishman we'd gotten to know here on our last trip. We had filmed him talking to Farrah for the documentary. He had a similar cancer that had also spread to his liver and he was undergoing a similar treatment. Farrah is a very private person, but the cancer had given her a feeling of having something in common with so many people.

"He died day before yesterday," Eileen said quietly. I caught my breath. Then I turned and saw the effect this news had on Farrah. She got very quiet and didn't say a word. He'd had the same kind of cancer she has, and she was so positive that he was beating it. He had been a beacon of hope for her.

Dr. Vogl came into the hotel room to check on Farrah around ten this morning. He was quite upset with the doctors back home. He said her liver was in good condition when she left here last June, and he couldn't understand how it had gotten into this kind of shape between then and now. He actually seemed angry about it. He's a man of few words, but you definitely knew how he was feeling. He was happy with the CT scan they did after the chemo embolization, however. It showed that the tumor that was causing the leg to swell had already shrunk by 30 percent, which is highly unusual. Her leg is already better this morning.

After that we got dressed, had breakfast, and made the hellish five-hour drive to the clinic. We made a bed in the back of the van for Farrah, who wasn't feeling very well, but she couldn't sleep. Little wonder. Mr. Carstens, the crotchety old driver from the clinic, had rented a VW van, which was so light and flimsy that you could feel every bump in the road. I actually felt so carsick that I had to take some of Farrah's nausea medicine.

We finally arrived around six o'clock and Dr. Jacob was waiting for us. She wanted to talk to Farrah about what Dr. Vogl had found and about the treatment plan she wants to start right away. She said Dr. Vogl had called her three times yesterday and three times this morning, he was so concerned about how things had progressed. She reiterated that the tumor on the lymph node in the lower abdomen was the size of a tennis ball, and that's why Farrah's leg was so swollen and she was having such pain. Dr. Vogl had put most of the chemo into the primary tumor and the one in the lymph node because they had to be treated aggressively. She has to go back in ten days for the full liver perfusion.

"It's not good, but I still have hope," Dr. Jacob said. "When I no longer have hope, I will tell you to get your affairs in order." At least that seemed more hopeful than what Dr. Vogl had said to me in private. Dr. Jacob says that Farrah has to stay as long as necessary to reduce the tumors and then come back four or five weeks afterward. Farrah said I can go home early, but I won't leave her. I can be just as stubborn, my friend.

*February 23, 2009*

I've been looking in on Farrah every so often. Tomorrow we go to Dr. Kiehling, who will put in a port so they don't have to keep trying to find a vein and repair the hernia in her abdomen that has occurred in the last few months, probably from all the vomiting. I just went over to see her and she was drifting off to sleep.

I called Mimmo to say I would come over for dinner tonight. He said (in Italian, of course) that his friend would be joining us.

"What friend?" I asked him.

"The one I told you about," he replied. He was talking about the girl he's been dating, the one he made it sound like he wasn't all that involved with. He told me over the phone a few weeks ago that he had told her I was his *"grande amore,"* and that when I came here, he would be seeing me. I can't imagine any woman taking that very well.

I said, "Mimmo, are you crazy? I don't want to have dinner with your girlfriend. You and I haven't even talked, and I've never met her." Then he said she had wanted to come (I'll bet) and that he couldn't really tell her she couldn't. I was kind of flabbergasted, so I just said, "Don't worry about it. I'll come another night."

He said to come for lunch tomorrow, but I told him I was going to Bad Tölz with Farrah to see Dr. Kiehling. I hung up, kind of surprised and disappointed, but what else is new? Honest to God, it seems I always get disappointed by men. I suppose I wanted it all on my terms. After all, he was my distraction from what I'm going through with Farrah. Maybe it's better this way. I can just write, and read, and spend time with Farrah. I keep remembering Dr. Vogl's solemn words: "Spend all the time you can with her." Everything happens for a reason.

### February 25, 2009

Farrah looked and sounded much better, although she was in some pain from the surgery yesterday. The pain got worse as the day went on, so they gave her a lot of pain medication, and she went to sleep early tonight.

### February 26, 2009

I couldn't sleep. I've woken up about every three hours. I kept thinking about the Mimmo thing. There's another woman in Mimmo's life and, frankly, it bothers me. Why can't I just be happy for him? It's better for him to have a German girlfriend who is here all the time. He needs someone in his life so he's not always alone with his dog. I guess I'm just being selfish and I need to pray about it; that I can open my heart and be happy for him.

What I seem to be getting hit over the head with is a lesson in "ego" and letting go. Everything has to change in life, but I, being a Taurus, cling to people and situations until my fingernails bleed. I hate change! It scares me. Always has. Yet everything is changing so rapidly around me these days. My best friend no longer resembles the Farrah I've always known and she's fighting for her life. And my own life continues to be in flux and filled with uncertainty. I feel like there's no foundation underneath me anymore.

### ❖ February 28, 2009

A story came out in the *Daily Mirror* in London and was printed here yesterday saying that Farrah is dying. I had to speak to a journalist here that Dr. Jacob knows and also to someone from *Entertainment Tonight* who called me.

"Of course it's not true," I told them. "She's here for her usual treatments and we're finishing the documentary." I said that this was another example of irresponsible journalism, and that if she were dying, wouldn't Ryan and her son be here with her? The scary part is that I'm afraid, at some point, it's going to be true. I'm walking a fine line. I don't want to be untruthful with anyone, but Farrah is not dying *at this moment*. I can't share with the journalists the fears that are deep in my heart. I have to share my optimism. We're keeping all of this away from Farrah. She doesn't need to be upset by any of this negative publicity.

### ❖ March 3, 2009

Today Dr. Jacob came in with Farrah's reports from the lab. Bad news and good news. The cancer cells have mutated and gotten much more aggressive. The chemo she had in L.A. clearly didn't work, and the cancer grew and spread. It's like this thing is an alien monster that nothing so far has been able to stop. But the good news is that the sensitivity testing showed that there are a number of substances that should work on her kind of cancer, and

Dr. Jacob is starting her on them immediately. Farrah continues to be in a lot of pain and hardly gets out of bed. She's on heavy pain medication, and we have to go back to Dr. Vogl on Thursday for another perfusion of the liver and the other tumors. Dr. Jacob feels very positive that the new treatment plan she's going to implement will make a big difference.

### March 5, 2009

We're in the van driving a million miles an hour on the way to Frankfurt for Farrah's procedure with Dr. Vogl. It's like being in the Indy 500, the way these people drive. I pray we'll make it there in one piece.

**Later**

We're on the way back, literally flying along the autobahn at breakneck speed in blinding rain. Mr. Carstens, our ancient German driver, ignores me every time I tentatively ask, "Aren't we going a little fast?" I'm too nervous to lie down and try to sleep even though it's after eleven o'clock and I'm exhausted. Farrah is sound asleep in the backseat. I'm glad the day is over for her and it went smoothly. I guess that's easy for me to say, considering I'm not the one who had to have her main artery sliced open and a long tube of wire threaded into her liver, where the chemo and antibody drugs were injected. She had to rest for four hours afterward in a recovery room to make sure the bleeding had stopped, and then we were allowed to leave.

I feel numbed by all of this. My friend no longer looks like herself. She now looks like a cancer victim: weak, gaunt, and without her glorious mane of hair. She looks like a little fragile bird. It's heartbreaking.

## ❧ *March 6, 2009*

We returned to the clinic yesterday. Today Dr. Jacob came into my room to talk about how things went.

"Dr. Vogl was unusually quiet," I told her. "He didn't say much. I don't think he was happy with what he found."

"No," she said. "He was very unhappy with the condition of the liver. There are so many tumors in the liver now, he says it's very serious and doesn't know if she will make it. But I have hopes that these other therapies will start to work and that the perfusion he did yesterday will shrink the tumors in the liver and the pelvic region."

"And if it doesn't work?"

"She will not have very much time," she answered solemnly.

Dr. Jacob said that Farrah knows the liver is serious but doesn't know how bad it is, and Dr. Jacob doesn't want her to know. I agree. Farrah has to have hope to keep fighting.

Maybe I'm starting to understand why this has happened with Mimmo. I need to be with my friend all the time and not be distracted by anything else. Dr. Vogl's words are still ringing in my ears: "Spend all the time you can with her." I can't believe this is happening. But despite it all I still have hopes for a miracle.

### ◈ March 10, 2009

Farrah's hernia site, where Dr. Kiehling operated, hasn't healed properly, and there's a large hematoma there. She went into the hospital yesterday for Dr. Kiehling to perform a second surgery. Now Dr. Jacob doesn't know how long it will be before she can have the next liver perfusion. It's starting to feel like we'll be here forever. We're booked to go back on the twenty-third, but I don't see that happening.

### ◈ March 11, 2009

Things are looking up. Last night Farrah was better. Our friend Dominick Dunne is here at the clinic, and he gave us some of his videos. We watched *The Two Mrs. Woodwards,* and ended up giggling about men in my past before going to sleep.

"This is fun," Farrah said. "Kind of like having a slumber party."

I felt like I had my girlfriend back for the moment. These times seem to be fewer and further apart.

### ◈ March 13, 2009

I don't know what got into Farrah today. She threw a bottle at the housekeeper and knocked everything off her table in a fit of

rage. Everyone is afraid to go into her room. I think it's a combination of the pain medication she's been on for so long now and
everything just building up in her over the past couple of years.
She's had to endure so many surgeries and procedures, so much
pain, so many indignities. I can't blame her for getting angry and
having to release it all. I came when I heard the ruckus and tried
to calm her down. "What's going on?" I asked. She was in pain
and she had been calling the nurses for an hour and couldn't get
their attention. She just lost it, understandably so. "Just don't throw
anything at me, Blanche," I teased. I've been calling her that since
one of our earlier trips here when she was hooked up to an IV and
couldn't move off her bed. After asking me to get her about ten
different things, I finally turned to her and said, "You're skating
on thin ice, Blanche. Don't be surprised if you find a rat on your
dinner tray tonight." It became a running joke for us: I called her
Blanche and I was Baby Jane.

◈ *March 22, 2009*

I feel like I'm in *Groundhog Day*. Each day just melds into the
next. Over a week has passed and nothing has changed that
much. Farrah has had ups and downs, and seems a little better
today, but she's still not well enough to fly home. She's so weak
and frail, and barely eats anything. They're giving her liquid nutrition through the IV now.

I'm feeling unbelievably depressed, like there's no end in sight.
I don't want to focus on myself when she's so ill, but I'm desperate

to get home. I miss my kids and my dogs so much, but most of all, at this moment, I miss Farrah. This has been the worst trip of all. At least during the others we were able to hang out, laugh, and have some fun times in the midst of all the seriousness.

Every week now is a roller coaster; one day she's better, the next she's worse. I never know what the day will hold when I wake in the morning. All I can do is pray.

## ❖ *March 27, 2009*

We're leaving tomorrow, finally! A real blizzard came in on Tuesday and it snowed like crazy for two full days. I was in heaven. Everything looked just like a Christmas card. The Germans are fed up with snow, but Farrah and I just sat and watched it coming down.

Growing up in Texas, we never had snow except for once on Christmas Eve in Nacogdoches when I was five. I remember standing at the window, waiting for my mother to arrive, and watching these beautiful snowflakes with awe. Farrah and I didn't say much as we sat there watching the snow; we were sort of hypnotized. I've never seen such large snowflakes, big lacy doilies floating down for hours on end.

At one point, she said, "You've given up so much of your life to do this for me. I don't know how I can ever thank you." I replied, "If I had a sister, I'd do it for her, and you're like my sister." I made my way through the lines hanging from the IV pole to hug her. It was one of the most intimate, tender moments we've ever had.

**Later**

I went over to Mimmo's for lunch and he was very sweet. He had his lunch with me after everyone left, and I told him I was leaving tomorrow and that I probably would not be coming back. I also told him Dr. Jacob is moving the clinic to the Black Forest near Stuttgart. I said it might be the last time we saw each other and he said, "No, it won't be the last time. You will either come back or I will come to L.A. in November."

I asked him what about his girlfriend and he said something I didn't quite understand, like he would simply tell her he was "going on vacation." He also said he'd never get married. He said he was fed up with working so hard and he was going to sell the restaurant and live somewhere else, where it was warm. I get the sense that he's still in love with me, and he works very hard at being strong because we're so far apart. But the bottom line is that it's over. And although I've been affected by it much more than I thought I'd be, I need to let it go. Sad . . .

Farrah had an ultrasound late this afternoon and Dr. Jacob said there was fluid in her liver and it had to be removed. She told Farrah she would deaden the area and she wouldn't feel anything. Then she stuck what looked like a five-inch needle in her stomach and Farrah literally screamed in pain. And that was just to deaden the area so she could stick a tube inside the liver and drain the excess fluid out. It looked God-awful. Afterward, back in her room, Farrah was in a lot of pain. They gave her some pain medication and we talked on the bed for a long time. It was as if she didn't want me to leave her.

❧ *March 28, 2009*

I can't believe we're on the plane to Los Angeles. I wasn't sure Farrah could make it, she was in such pain and so weak, but somehow we managed to get her together, packed, and into the car.

Paparazzi were parked outside on the street in a black Porsche SUV and followed us to the Munich airport. We'd alerted the Lufthansa VIP people who were meeting us, and they had the police there. I got out first and immediately spotted a paparazzo down the street taking pictures of the car and the waiting wheelchair. Farrah stayed inside the car while the police chased him away. Then the guy in the black Porsche pulled up behind us, and I had to tell the police he was the one who had followed us from the clinic. They chased him away as well. They'd never be able to do that in L.A. They'd scream about their First Amendment rights and the next day they'd hire Gloria Allred to represent them.

We got Farrah out and into the wheelchair while the Lufthansa ladies held up blankets around her in case the paparazzi were somewhere around with long-range lenses. We got inside without incident, through the VIP terminal, and onto the plane. Farrah was in a lot of pain, so I gave her a pain shot and she's sleeping now. The problem is that the paparazzi from Munich will have alerted people in Los Angeles and I'm afraid there will be a slew of them waiting for us. It's not so easy to avoid them at LAX because they can come right into the terminal and there's no other way out that I know of. We'll have to see if the Lufthansa reps meeting us can come up with something.

❧ *March 29, 2009*

It was quite something at the airport last night. It all went smoothly until we got through customs, and suddenly we were ambushed by paparazzi, who got the picture they've been waiting for: Farrah in a wheelchair. We tried our best to surround her and get her into the car, but I'm sure they got what they wanted.

"Are you guys proud of yourselves?" I yelled at the one with the video camera. "How do you sleep at night, you slimy vermin?!" Honest to God, I really wanted to grab his camera and smash it on the ground, but I somehow resisted. I figured this was not the time to get arrested.

❧ *April 5, 2009*

Dr. Piro put Farrah in the hospital four days ago. She's in a lot of pain from the hematoma, and her blood tests weren't good, so he needs to give her a transfusion. When I saw her today, I was shocked at how she looked, so gaunt and pale and drawn. I've thought that a couple of times before, but she never looked like this. It really frightens me.

❖ *April 6, 2009*

My phone started ringing at 8 A.M. this morning and didn't stop all day. I literally didn't have time to get out of my nightgown until tonight, when I changed to pajamas. I think I must have had over fifty phone calls about Farrah and all these crazy stories in the press reporting that she's in a coma and hovering near death. Finally, Dr. Piro made a statement to the media, but instead of quieting it down and making it go away, it just kept growing. The Associated Press reported that the cancer had gone to her liver, like it had just happened, when the *Enquirer* reported it over a year ago. It was like writing that Abe Lincoln had just been shot. What is wrong with all these people? It's become a feeding frenzy.

❖ *April 7, 2009*

I took my dog Lolita for her surgery this morning and then went up to the hospital to see Farrah. She looked much better today and was more lucid. Dr. Piro is cutting down on the pain medication and she's not completely out of it all the time. She's still not even close to being herself, but at least I am beginning to see a glimmer of hope. I went to Poquito Mas and got us nachos in hopes she might eat something. She promised she would if I went to get them, but she only had a bite. She promised to eat more later.

The vet's assistant called and said Lolita was doing fine and in recovery. Then he told me that they had sent the tumor for another biopsy because it was deeper than they had thought and had blood vessels going from it. Fatty tissue tumors, which the doctor had thought that it was, don't generally have blood vessels attached. That's all I needed to hear to throw me into a full-scale panic attack. What if it's malignant? I tried to get some encouraging words out of him, but I wasn't at all satisfied. He said they had to send it in to the lab to rule out malignancy, but he didn't leave me feeling very reassured. He also told me that her left hip joint has some dysplasia, and that's why she seems to be having trouble with her left leg. Please, God, don't let anything happen to my dog. I can't bear it. Not now. Not any time soon. I just can't bear any more loss right now.

I picked her up this evening and she was very quiet and subdued. She's sleeping on the living room rug now. I curled up beside her and just lay there.

### April 9, 2009

I went to the hospital to meet Ryan and bring Farrah home. We disguised her and got her into the wheelchair and out the back door of the hospital to avoid any paparazzi. She went straight to bed and to sleep when we got back to the apartment, and Ryan and I watched the documentary footage. We really wanted it to be great, but it wasn't what we had hoped it would be. Initially Ryan was a lot more critical than I was, because I needed to think about it for a while, but then what I realized was that it was very confusing.

It always worried me that Farrah was so positive she could control it all. Whenever I voiced my concerns she'd say, "Don't worry, I have final approval. We'll go into the edit room and work on it. It'll be fun." But I knew she was getting sicker and that she wasn't going to be able to physically do what she would have to do to ensure that it would turn out how she envisioned. I don't know what will happen.

❧ *April 10, 2009*

Finally, Lolita's vet called to say the second tumor was malignant, but he quickly pointed out that it wasn't the kind of cancer that spreads throughout the body or metastasizes. It will, however, more than likely come back unless Lolita has radiation or a second surgery that's very invasive. He doesn't recommend radiation for her because she's almost nine years old and has Addison's disease, and radiation wouldn't necessarily ensure that the tumor won't come back. He said the second surgery would get all the cells in the surrounding tissue and would give her a better chance of the tumor not recurring. But even that wouldn't be for sure.

I'm so confused. My instinct is not to put Lolita through this torturous surgery and just start a lot of prayer work for her. My minister says that animals really respond to prayer. She's been sleeping on the bed again. She can only put her front paws up, and I have to lift her bottom up. I just want to slow down the clock and have her live for many more years, but that wouldn't be possible even without the tumor. She's already nine and big dogs like her don't have such a long life span. I just want it not to be real; a figment of my imagination. By bedtime, I felt beat up and numb with depression. Why am I surrounded by cancer?

### ❖ *April 13, 2009*

I cooked Easter dinner for the kids last night: fried chicken, macaroni and cheese, black-eyed peas, and cornbread. Good Texas food. I took some over to Farrah today, and Ryan got her to eat a little. She's hardly been eating anything.

Farrah was strong enough today to have a meeting with her attorney and business manager, Bernie Francis. When Bernie asked her who she wanted in charge creatively of the documentary, she very clearly said "Ryan" and succinctly explained why. She sat up in bed and said, "Ryan and I have been together so many years and I trust him to know exactly how I think and what I would want creatively." I was so relieved. At least I know that he will protect her and oversee something that she will be proud of.

Afterward, she, Ryan, and I watched Dominick Dunne's show, *Power, Privilege and Justice,* on television, and she was able to watch the entire show before she went to sleep. We had a really nice evening together. I felt encouraged when I left.

◈ *April 17, 2009*

Tonight Farrah, Ryan, and I were all piled on her bed watching the cut of the documentary that Ryan and I had already seen and that we—and NBC—were disappointed in. Farrah watched the entire thing intently. Afterward, she said very clearly, "You guys have a lot of work to do." Then she turned over and went to sleep.

◈ *April 18, 2009*

It's been a long, stressful week. Farrah signed all the papers that the attorney and business manager needed her to sign so that Ryan can take over creative control of the documentary while she isn't able to oversee it.

Ryan went to his wrap party tonight, so I told him I'd stay with Farrah. The nurse was there, but it didn't seem right to leave Farrah alone without one of us. I made her some toast, the kind her dad makes where you put dabs of butter on white bread and put it in the toaster oven. She ate a few bites, but that was all. The doctor ordered IV nutrition for her today and she has it dripping into her twenty-four hours a day. She's so much thinner now than she was in the hospital; it looks as if I could get my finger and thumb around her arm. She's so weak that she can barely get up by herself.

I talked to Dr. Piro about it today. He said that if she started to gain a little weight and strength he could start her back on some of the cancer drugs, but at the moment she can't tolerate anything. It scares me that it could be only a matter of time now. I hope I'm wrong; I hope she hasn't given up. How could she not at some point? How much suffering can a body go through before all the fight is gone? I think those two surgeries and the liver procedure and the accompanying pain on top of the chemo she'd had here were just too much for her. It doesn't seem possible that it was almost two years ago that the cancer returned and she made that first trip to Germany. It seems like yesterday that we were all there. It had been such a successful trip, and we left with high hopes that she was going to beat this. And now . . .

I lay on the bed with her for a long time tonight. She was in and out of sleep, and I just lay there thinking and staring at the muted television screen. Finally, for the first time in weeks, I cried. Not the wracking sobs I feel somewhere deep inside me, just moist, silent tears sliding down my cheeks. The Farrah that I've known for so long is no longer there. I'm losing my best friend; in many ways I've already lost her. I'm grieving for that loss. How do I accept that we'll never go shopping again or get manicures or make pecan pies at Christmas? Or commiserate about our children, our men, our little aches and pains? Everything is always so much more fun when she is there.

### ❖ April 26, 2009

I'm trying to catch up with everything. We met all Friday afternoon with Doug Vaughan, the NBC exec, who flew out from

New York for the day, and Sandy Gleysteen, the producer they've brought on board to try to pull this mess together. Both Ryan and I liked Doug and Sandy very much and feel like we're all on the same page, to make something that Farrah will be as proud of as if she'd been able to oversee it herself.

I went over to the apartment yesterday morning to film Redmond coming to visit Farrah. He's still in jail in the Twin Towers, but they let him come to see his mom for a couple of hours. He was accompanied by two sheriffs, who literally waited inside the door of Farrah's room while Redmond saw her. They took his handcuffs off so she wouldn't see them, but his ankles were still shackled. It nearly broke my heart to see him like that. The first couple of times he went into her room she was barely awake, but then later she woke up and was able to talk with him. I didn't film anything with her, just Redmond lying on the bed with her from a distance in the darkened room. I don't want to film her anymore like this. It doesn't feel right. I haven't filmed anything close on her for a while now. I know she wouldn't want to be remembered like this, so frail and small and sick.

Ryan and I also filmed an interview with Redmond that we hope to put in the documentary, because he needs to be seen as who he really is: a very sweet, smart kid with a drug problem, not some messed-up criminal. My heart went out to him. How it must feel to see his mother like this and to have to go back to jail. We're hoping he'll be transferred to the Impact Program for addicts at Wayside and not sent to prison, which it seems is still a very real possibility. After we filmed, I made him some bacon and scrambled eggs and had a nice talk with him. It's the first time I've seen him sober and clean in so long. It was bizarre, because the lady sheriff stayed in the small kitchen with us, and actually we all ended up having a really good conversation. She told him it was up to him now to change his life. I'm sure that's what everyone says, but it was interesting coming from her. She seemed to have a real understanding of drug addiction and was surprisingly compassionate. Funny, as she stood there in her brown uniform, her arms crossed and her gun at her side.

### April 27, 2009

I went over to Farrah's. Ryan was there. We were lying on the bed, and when I said I needed to go home to feed my dogs, she said, so clearly, "Do you have to go? This is so much fun."

I said, "No, I don't have to go. I'll stay." I got her to eat a few bites of food, but not much. She said, again, "This is fun." I wonder if she's remembering the fun we used to have, the good times. Farrah was more awake and alert than I've seen her in quite a while. Then she started to feel some pain and asked for her pain medication and was soon sleeping. Sweet dreams, honey.

### April 30, 2009

Everything is moving really quickly. I'm feeling scared and overwhelmed with all the work in front of us. Ryan and I have to do the *Today* show on Monday, satellite interviews, *People* magazine, and this screening at the Paley Center. It's all happened at once and I'm terrified. It all seems surreal, the documentary coming out when Farrah is so ill. It feels like maybe it's disrespectful of her condition, but I guess at this point we can't stop it. NBC had already committed to an air date. It wasn't supposed to be like this. The story was meant to have a different ending. Farrah should be doing the *Today* show, not me and Ryan.

## May 1, 2009

I went to see Farrah tonight. She was more awake and coherent for a little while. She smiled when she saw me. I told her how much I missed her the last two days and that the reason I hadn't come was because I was sick. I told her I'd made macaroni and cheese and chicken matzo ball soup, and she lit up. I also told her Dr. Jacob was coming with this new antibody and that she had to keep her faith. She took my hand and said, "Maybe this will turn everything around." I lay with her for a while after she had her pain medication and read to her from *Science and Health,* the Christian Science book by Mary Baker Eddy. I read her a couple of prayers, which she liked, and then some stories of healing that people had experienced from just reading the book. She listened and seemed to really like it. I'm going to try to do that every day now. I'm starting to just see her in God's light and love and believe that there can be a miracle. I can't see her as dying, no matter what the medical world says. I realized that I, of all people, can't give up on her yet. Maybe I'm in denial, but I have to practice this new belief that I'm reading about, the power of God to do what might to human eyes seem impossible.

### May 7, 2009

Ryan and I got the cut of the show and watched it at my house because it wouldn't work in any of Farrah's machines. We both thought it was pretty good, and we made notes, but nothing major. Afterward, we went back to Farrah's. I made her a grilled cheese sandwich, which she ate a few bites of, and she drank some tea. Ryan and I hung out on the bed with her for a while. He's so sweet and gentle with her. She seemed a little more like Farrah than usual. She even made sense until she got her next injection of pain medication, and then she wanted to know "where her dogs were." An interesting question since she doesn't have any, bless her heart. She went off to sleep and I went home.

### May 13, 2009

Tonight was the premiere of *Farrah's Story* at the Paley Center in Beverly Hills. I felt like pinching myself; everything has been happening so fast and furiously. Doug Vaughan introduced me, and I made a short speech introducing the documentary. I was nervous about what the reaction would be, but I was completely blown away by the response. Many people in the audience literally cried all through the film, and afterward everyone was raving about it.

I was incredibly proud to be a part of it, but I almost felt like I didn't deserve the praise I was getting. I wanted to say, "But all I really did was hold the camera." I almost can't believe that I actually shot most of this film. But the person who really deserves the credit is Sandy Gleysteen for working so tirelessly to pull it together in time, as well as Ryan for his creative input. And most of all Farrah, for being willing to share her journey and her courage. She's such an inspiration and has touched people so profoundly. I can't believe it all started with her filming her doctors that day at UCLA when they told her the cancer had come back. And then she handed the camera to me in Germany and asked me to film. Who would have thought it would turn into this? All that was sadly missing was Farrah. This was really her evening.

### May 15, 2009

We watched the documentary at Farrah's last night, just Ryan, Farrah, and me. She really liked it. She said that she thought we did a great job. She wasn't very comfortable, but she made it through the entire thing. I have to say, seeing it again, that it's really an amazing show, and so well done. Dr. Piro came over to watch the end of it with us.

After it was over, I asked her, "So, did you really like it?"

She answered very clearly, "I liked it very, very, very, very, *very* much."

God, was I relieved. Then I asked, jokingly, "So you're still speaking to me after seeing the bald shot?"

She said again that she liked it and thought we'd done a great job. I'd really been sweating that one, just in case she wouldn't have wanted it in, but I think she sees how powerful and how honest it was. Dr. Piro echoed what Sandy had said earlier, that it was extremely important for any woman who had ever lost her hair to chemo to see Farrah show such courage and power over losing probably the most famous head of hair in the world. And instead of being a victim, she had shaved it herself rather than wait for the chemo to take it.

Today, I'm so tired. It's more brain tired than physically tired. I'm feeling overwhelmed by all the phone calls and e-mails, but I guess I should be happy.

*They were the golden couple.*

*When they walked into a room, you just knew it from the looks on everyone's faces. The whole room would brighten up the minute they arrived. No matter what the party was—whether it was just sitting around the house and having drinks or a black tie New Year's Eve party—it was always more fun with them there.*

*This photo was taken at the party I threw for Farrah's birthday on February 2, 1991. They were always a great combination. He told stories and held court, while she was ever the willing and enthusiastic audience. Farrah played off him and they'd banter back and forth.*

*They had their ups and downs—there's no denying that. But sometimes you feel like two people are made for each other, and that's how I always felt about them. Through all their struggles they were there for each other, this perfect match that seemed like they'd been through everything together twice.*

&#10086; *May 17, 2009*

Melanie Griffith has called me about this man named Howard Wills, who apparently has done amazing healings on people. He's in town from Hawaii, where he lives, and she urged me to get in touch with him and have him see Farrah. The first time she called, I honestly thought, "I can't deal with one more healer who doesn't end up healing." Finally, this morning I decided to call him, and while I was speaking to him, I got chills and started to cry. There was something very powerful about his voice, with his distinctly southern accent, that convinced me to give it a try. I made arrangements to pick him up where he was staying, which happened to be two blocks away from Farrah's apartment. I also asked Ryan if he was okay with it, which he was.

Howard was waiting downstairs when I drove up. I knew it had to be him. He was tall, with long gray hair pulled back in a ponytail, piercing blue eyes, and was dressed totally in white. He looked rather ageless, but I guessed him to be in his late forties or early fifties. We drove to Farrah's and I took him upstairs. She was sleeping soundly, and the nurse said she'd been in pain, so she had just given her some pain medication. Howard said he would just sit in the chair across the room and do his work. Farrah slept, while he just gazed steadily at her for what seemed about an hour. I lay down on the bed beside her. I figured I might as well soak up some healing rays in the process.

When he was done with whatever it was he was doing, he stood up and we left the room. I told him I hadn't been feeling so great the last few days, and he said, "Just stand there and tell me what you feel." He stood a few feet away from me with his right arm outstretched and his right hand pointed toward me, and sort of rocked back and forth with his eyes closed. I felt as if there was an electrical current going through my body. "Smell your skin," he instructed me. "What do you smell?"

"It smells like a magnet," I said.

"You'll feel better now," he said. I offered to drive him back to his hotel, but he said he'd walk, and that he'd come back tomorrow if I wanted him to. After he left, I noticed that I felt much better: calmer and clearer.


*May 18, 2009*


It was all surreal. Last night I got a call from NBC asking if I would do the *Today* show at seven thirty Eastern, which would mean that I'd have to go on the air at four thirty our time. I was incredulous, but I agreed to do it, in spite of the fact that today is my birthday.

We arrived at the NBC studios at 2:30 A.M. Farrah's longtime friend and makeup artist, Mela, did my makeup and hair, and I was ready to go on live at four fifteen. Ryan had agreed to do it from home in Malibu by phone. From his bed. Lucky him! They asked me to do MSNBC afterward, so I did a quick live interview, then got into the car, went to the CBS studios, and did *ET* and *The Insider*. I was home by eight o'clock. I took two Ativan and tried to sleep, somewhat successfully, in between the doorbell ringing and the dogs barking.

I woke up and hurriedly pulled myself together to go to Sandy Gallin's house for my birthday dinner. I hadn't planned to do anything other than have dinner with my kids, but Sandy sweetly offered to have a few friends over for me at the last minute. Lowell, Sandy's cook, made all my southern favorites: fried chicken, turnip greens, macaroni and cheese, corn pudding, coleslaw, barbecue ribs, and, for dessert, besides a fabulous chocolate birthday cake, there was banana pudding, peach cobbler, and blueberry crumble. He packed a bag full of food for us to take back to Farrah. Ryan came, and all of our friends came up and told us how much they loved the documentary. But I felt like there was a big hole in my heart because Farrah wasn't there.

Besides a dozen or so of my friends, all my kids, Ashley, Sean, and Kimberly, showed up. I was really moved; spending an evening with the "old folks" probably isn't the most fun thing in the world. I got some lovely birthday presents, but the most special was the birthday card from my daughter. It read,

*Dearest Mom,*

*I cannot thank you enough for letting me stay here. You mean so much to me, and the more time I spend with you, the more I respect and love you. I feel bad every day that we went so long not being close. Hopefully, we are making up for lost time. Happy b-day, and I will miss you so much. Who will scratch my back and keep me on a spiritual path in London?*

*Love you loads,*
*Kim*

This healing of my relationship with my daughter is such a wonderful gift that I owe to Farrah. This experience with her has made me a more open, unconditionally loving and patient person, and I believe that has helped to heal the breach between me and my daughter.

◈ *May 20, 2009*

Last night I watched the Lakers game with Ryan and Farrah. She was much more alert and talkative. I started to have hope again. I know I keep saying it, but I don't know how else to describe it: it feels like I'm riding a roller coaster. One day down, next day up.

Tonight I went over to Farrah's to meet Howard. Farrah didn't even know Howard was there. He just sat in the corner for a long time and silently prayed. I lay on the bed beside her and fell asleep. After he left, she woke up, and I told her he'd been coming to see her and praying for her.

"Is it okay if he comes back tomorrow?" I asked her.

"Yes, please," she whispered. I kissed her goodnight and left.

◈ *May 21, 2009*

We had such an amazing experience this afternoon. Howard came over to Farrah's again. Ryan and I sat in the living room with him for a few minutes. I was nervous about how Ryan would receive him, but surprisingly, he was really comfortable with him. Howard told us about some of the people he had healed. He said it was all about God working through him, and how important it was to love Farrah. "You just have to love her, and be positive, and believe she can get well," he told Ryan. "The words you speak are very powerful," he added. "I can do that," Ryan said enthusiastically.

I asked Howard if he'd ever healed people with addictions. He said people use drugs to numb their pain, and that the pain comes not only from the present day but from their lineage, and that he healed the entire family through the previous generations. I told him my mother had been a drug addict, that my two sons had suffered from addiction, and that I had ongoing health problems. He led me through a prayer about healing and forgiving my mother and asking her to forgive me. I started to cry during it. I cried even harder when he did the same process for my children. Afterward I felt so light and free, like a terrible burden had been lifted from me psychically.

What really surprised me was Ryan's response—he was so sweet and compassionate, I didn't feel at all uncomfortable crying in front of him. I somehow felt like the whole experience made us even closer. I feel like we've bonded in our love and concern for Farrah and that we're all very much like a family.

Then we took Howard into Farrah's room. She wasn't aware that he was there at first. She was feeling terrible. She threw up several times and was in a lot of pain. I lay on the bed with her while Howard sat in the chair in the corner. Then Ryan brought Howard over to Farrah and introduced him. She kind of perked up with interest and actually began talking softly with him. She said her knee hurt and I asked him if he could work on it. He stood a couple of feet away and held out his hand toward her knee, and after a minute he asked her, "How does it feel now?" "Better," she said. He asked, "Where else do you have pain?" She pointed to her abdomen. Again he held out his hand, this time toward her stomach. After a minute, he asked how she felt, and she said, "Much better. My body feels so relaxed."

"He worked on Ryan, too," I told her.

"I wondered why he was so quiet," she teased.

I laughed. The old Farrah humor was back.

"He's working on Redmond, too, honey."

"Can you help him?" she asked Howard.

"Yes, I certainly can," he answered. "I'm going to work on all of you, and you're going to get better. I want you to believe that. You can get well and be healthy again."

I thought it was time for me to leave them alone, so I kissed her good-bye and said I was going to feed the dogs.

"I can't thank you enough," she said softly.

"Just get well. That's all I want," I said. I kissed her again and left the room.

Ryan was on the terrace talking with Howard's wife, a pretty, hippie-looking young woman named Ahava. I talked to them for a few minutes and then left for home and my doggies. I felt like something very special had happened this evening. I so very much want to believe that Farrah can get well. I don't know how it could happen, but I feel like with God, anything is possible.

### May 23, 2009

I met Howard at Farrah's this afternoon. She seemed genuinely glad to see him. She is clearly stronger, especially her voice. I let them talk alone until Dr. Piro arrived to see how she was doing. He felt she was doing much better, too, although he probably thinks it has more to do with the antibiotics than the healing work. I know in my heart that Howard is doing something miraculous. I believe he is actually helping to heal their whole family dynamic, which I'm sure has a lot to do with anyone getting sick. I know that for me it has played a huge part in my health. When Ashley or Sean was drinking or using drugs and I was fearing for their lives, I was a wreck physically. That kind of stress and the hopelessness that accompanies it is devastating to a mother. Marianne Williamson once told me an old saying: "You are only as happy as your least happy child." I know that for me it's true and

I know it's true for Farrah. She loves Redmond so much, and to see him struggling with drug addiction has been a huge emotional and, I believe, physical trauma for her. I think Howard is helping her let go of a lot of emotional baggage and that perhaps she can be free to heal now.

I also see a huge difference in Ryan. I think he really gets from Howard how important it is to be loving and positive with Farrah and he's doing it. One thing I do know: no matter what the ups and downs have been, this man loves her with all his heart. I feel different as well. I feel this tremendous love for her when I'm around her. Not that I didn't always love her, but this is different somehow. It seems to fill my complete being, and it's not just with her. It's with everyone and everything. Of course, I have my doubts. Can this man or anything else really heal all these tumors that have taken over her body? Is this too good to be true? I try not to entertain these thoughts and get back to my faith. I can't afford to hold on to any negative thoughts or feelings, especially now.

❖ *May 25, 2009*

I went over to Farrah's around seven thirty. She was awake, but not very happy. Ryan was his usual loud, energetic self, asking her if she wanted to go out on the terrace in the wheelchair, or watch a Dominick Dunne murder mystery, or have some barbecue chicken and mashed potatoes. She opted out of all three, so he turned his attention to helping the two nurses attempt to put together the bed bars to keep her from getting out of bed and falling. She kept moaning softly like she was really uncomfortable.

Shortly after I got there, Howard arrived and came into her room. She seemed to brighten when she saw him. I told him I had brought over the coconut oil he'd asked me to get, so he showed Ryan how to rub it in very gently onto her back and down her spine. Howard took some of the oil, warmed it in his hands, and gently began rubbing her arms, talking to her all the while in his southern drawl. She was answering him very lucidly in a much stronger voice than she's had for ages. He had her move her arms around and stretch them and she did it, making punching motions. We were astonished, especially since she's hardly been able to raise food to her mouth.

Then he stood over her and raised his hands and started that strange rocking motion with his head while looking upward. After several minutes, he asked, "How do you feel?"

"Much better," she said.

"You see," he said. "You're getting well. You'll be playing tennis in no time."

"Do you really think that could happen?" she asked.

"Without a doubt," he answered firmly.

He continued rubbing oil on her while we talked about Texas and chicken-fried steak and turnip greens. I said I would make some this week and bring it over for all of us.

He said good-bye to her, and as he left the room, I leaned over to kiss her good-bye as well. "I love you, honey," she said softly, looking rather exhausted by this point.

"I love you very much," I said.

She kind of grimaced, and when I asked her what was wrong, she said, "I'm a little nauseous."

"Shall I call Howard?" I asked.

She held her hand up and begged, "No . . . please!" She clearly meant she'd had enough for one night! Healing can be exhausting.

### May 28, 2009

I went to the gynecologist at UCLA for my Pap smear. The last one in Germany was inconclusive. I get so nervous each time I have to have one now. I remember always admonishing Farrah in the years before she got cancer that she needed to slow down and take care of herself. She was always putting everyone else first and not taking time to rest and recuperate from stressful periods. She went through such a painful and exhausting time when her mother was dying in Texas. She practically lived in her hospital room for several months taking care of her. She ignored what should have been danger signals about her own health, and eventually she was diagnosed with cancer.

Now I feel like I'm doing the same thing. I guess that's exactly what Howard is talking about. I feel like I haven't been able to take any time for myself in too long. But how can I? There's always so much in front of me to do. I feel like I desperately need a week's vacation, but I can't do it now. I can't go away and leave Farrah for a week. I'm doing exactly what I was always fussing at her for doing, pushing myself unmercifully. But I don't know how to stop.

I stopped by Farrah's on the way home. Ryan had just arrived and we went in to see her. She wasn't feeling so well. I asked her if it was all right if Howard came by later and she said it was.

"I'll be back later," I said.

"Are you leaving?" she asked.

"Yes, unless you don't want me to," I answered with a smile.

"I don't want you to," she said, smiling back.

"Okay, I'll stay then," I said. "Shall I make you some watermelon juice, like we had on our vacation in Mexico?" I thought the memory of that happy time would lift her spirits.

"Maybe just some watermelon . . . ," she answered with a feeble smile. "But I think I'll have it later. Maybe I'll sleep now." Her eyes started to close. I kissed her gently on the forehead and quietly left the room.

When Howard came by, he showed Ryan how to do the kind of healing work he'd been doing on Farrah. He whispered to Ryan some thoughts he should hold in his head and his heart as he was doing it, and as Ryan held his hands close to Farrah, tears started to roll down his face. Farrah was completely present in the moment with him. He leaned down very close to her and spoke to her gently, asking her forgiveness, and she put her arms out and held him close. I was crying as well, watching this exchange that was more powerful than any love scene in a movie, because it was real.

It's clear that these two people love each other with a love that is very deep, very special, and lasting beyond life and death. I feel like there has been an incredible healing between the two

of them and that it includes Redmond as well. If only God will
grant her a miracle and she can recover so that she can fully enjoy
this healing of her family.

◈ *June 4, 2009*

I'm on pins and needles waiting for Ryan to call. Dr. Piro is
supposed to give us the results of Farrah's CT scan yesterday. They
took her to the hospital by private ambulance so Dr. Piro could do
the scan and she could have a blood transfusion. He wants to keep
her there a couple of days and try to build her up a little. I was kind
of pissed off last night that the scan was done in the early afternoon and somehow the radiologist left before he and Dr. Piro
could talk. Here we are, waiting nervously to find out these important results, which are available as soon as the scan is done, and it
somehow falls through the cracks. Things like this drive me crazy.
I woke up at five this morning, so stressed thinking about it that I
couldn't go back to sleep. When I left the hospital last night, Farrah seemed so fragile. I couldn't get it out of my mind.

Ryan just called in tears. The scans are terrible, he said. The
cancer is rampant in her liver and she has fluid in her lungs and a
bacterial infection. How much can she withstand?

I'm calling the doctor now. I'm in shock. I was so hoping that
Howard had brought a miracle with him. There was so much
healing going on in every other way, except in her poor body, apparently. I want to cry my eyes out, but I can't yet. I have to get
dressed and go see her. I have to think if there's something else we

can do. I won't give up until I have to. How can this happen in this way? She's seemed so much more present and alert lately. She's been so funny. Last night I called the nurse to see if Farrah wanted any Mexican food, because I was going to stop at El Cholo, our favorite Mexican restaurant, near the hospital. I didn't expect her to want anything, but I asked anyway.

"Alana's going to El Cholo," the nurse told her. "She wants to know if you want anything."

In the background I heard Farrah say, very matter-of-factly, "Alana knows what I want." Of course I did. I knew she would want a ground beef enchilada, a ground beef taco, and a green corn tamale. I got enough Mexican food for an army. She only ate a few bites, but she loved it. Our friend Mela arrived, and we had a little girls' night in her room.

I said, "I started to bring margaritas."

Farrah immediately said, "Why didn't you?"

Yesterday afternoon, Ryan had gotten her into the wheelchair for the first time and taken her out on the balcony for a few minutes. They called me from there, and she left me a voice mail message in her weak little voice. "I love you very much. I love you *very* much," she said. I got all teary when I heard it. I'll save that message forever if I can figure out how.

I went over later, and the two of them were so funny together. I asked the nurse why Farrah's knee was still so sore. She'd fallen and cut it several weeks ago and had a lot of stitches, but it didn't seem to be healing. Farrah said dryly, "Ryan ran into me with the wheelchair." We all had a good laugh. It was another "bacon sandwich" moment. Mela came over and we all lay on the bed with Farrah and talked. Howard arrived and did some of his healing work with her alone. I finally left, feeling really hopeful, around ten.

And now? I don't know what to do. I feel like I should be able to do something. I should be able to save her: find someone, find a cure, call Dr. Jacob, get her back here, *something*! Another healer? I feel desperate. I feel like I'm failing my friend. I can't just do *nothing*. There has to be more. There has to be something we haven't tried. There has to be that miracle that we always talked about. Doesn't there?

Maybe there comes a time when there is nothing more to do . . . I don't know.

### June 5, 2009

I spoke to Dr. Piro today. It's not quite as bad as Ryan's interpretation. He explained that the cancer has advanced somewhat, but that the pressing problem now is the fluid in her abdomen and lungs and the infection that still hasn't cleared up. The newest development is that the port is infected, and they have to surgically remove it this afternoon and put something temporary in its place until the infection heals. He doesn't feel any of these things are life threatening. It's rather a matter of taking care of each of them in the hospital, and hopefully, she'll be home early next week. He doesn't see anything horrible happening in the very near future, but it all seems to be piling up.

Howard has been calling to find out the results. I told him

about everything and said we were all very disappointed. I guess we'd expected this miracle healing. I asked him why Farrah hadn't had an instantaneous healing, like so many others had experienced from his work. He said, "Sometimes these things take time. She's been going through a lot for a long time and it's taken its toll on her. The work I've been doing with her has helped her to release a lot of old stuff. Her spirit has to heal and her body will follow. Don't give up, no matter what the doctors and the tests say. Just love her and get her to eat and build back her strength, and don't give up."

I am not giving up, but in my heart I wonder if it's still possible for her to rally one more time. She's a far cry right now from the strong, resilient, fighting Farrah who always bounced back no matter what. I feel sad, but not hopeless. I know there has been a tremendous spiritual healing with Farrah and with Ryan, and I believe even Redmond, although he's not here. I can't give up believing there can still be a miracle, even in the face of what seems to be grim reality. I worry about Ryan and Redmond if the worst happens. I know they'll be devastated. We all will. But after all, she's Red's mom and has been Ryan's love for over thirty years. I'll be there for them in any way I can. I feel like we've all become family now, bonded together in loving Farrah.

*June 7, 2009*

I went to the hospital yesterday. Ryan had been there for several hours. She had another surgery yesterday to remove the port.

She was very weak and still, barely able to speak from all the medications. I held her hand and stroked her head. I've noticed that her hair is growing back nicely, and that seems like a good sign. Ryan stood at the foot of her bed. "Are you comfortable?" he asked. She couldn't manage to get any words out, but she laughed. Just a tiny little smile/laugh that said, "Comfortable? Are you crazy? Do I look comfortable?" We all laughed with her. She still has her sense of humor.

### June 8, 2009

Mimmo called this morning. He calls once a week and asks how I am, how is Farrah, how are my dogs, Lolita and Bliss, etc., etc., etc. I told him as well as I could, since I haven't been practicing my Italian anymore, that I returned his call the other day, and when the machine at his home answered, it said something like "You have reached Mimmo and Nina . . ." I hung up without leaving a message, but it struck me that she's obviously living with him. He said that she stays there a lot and something about her cell phone not working. I felt like maybe it was finally time to just close this door.

"You have a girlfriend," I said. "We won't be seeing each other again, so I don't see any reason for you to continue to call me."

"But aren't we friends?" he replied. I wanted to say, "No, you jerk. You have a girlfriend, and I'm not interested in having another *friend*. And I don't like the way you handled things between us." But instead I simply explained that our romance was over, he had a new *amore,* and I didn't see any reason for us to keep talking. He was very taken aback, but finally accepted it. He said, "Ciao," and so did I, and we hung up.

I felt relieved and sad at the same time. It needed to end; it needed closure. I still have some resentment toward him, and I have to work on forgiving him and letting it go. Our romance served its purpose for a period of time, but it had nowhere to go and I suppose we both knew it. Perhaps if I'd been in love with him, things could have been different. I would have made more of an effort to be with him. I guess his practicality got the best of him. She was there and I wasn't. Better to love the one you're with than be with the one you love. Anyway, it's over, I'm alone, but there's so much going on in my life, it's the last thing I can think about. Sometimes I feel lonely, and it would be nice to have someone to share my life with, but if it's meant to be, then it will be. Meanwhile, I have a lot to deal with, and so does Farrah.

### June 9, 2009

Ryan called from the hospital last night so excited. He was with Farrah and they'd just finished watching the Lakers game. She was a little stronger and much more lucid. He said they had a wonderful time together, and he asked her to marry him! She said yes!

I screamed with joy. Wouldn't that be wonderful? The two of them belong together. Marianne Williamson said she could marry them since she's a minister. I started thinking about finding her a beautiful white nightgown and that Mela better start working on a wig. Maybe I'm just a hopeless romantic, but I can't help thinking that this would give her a boost and get her to rally, to rise once again like the phoenix, as she's done so many times before. And Ryan has really changed since he's worked with Howard. He's so gentle and loving with her. That's what she needs. Maybe she always has. Just to be loved and nourished and cared for by the man she's loved for so many years.

## June 10, 2009

I just lay down to meditate. I wasn't feeling well at all. I'd been going through some of the entries in my diary of when Farrah and I were at the clinic and suddenly got incredibly sad. I realized that we'd never be back there again. Even if by some miracle Farrah should get better, Dr. Jacob is moving her clinic to a completely different area, outside of Stuttgart. It'll be in one of the least attractive parts of Germany, if Stuttgart is any indication. So I'll never see Bad Wiessee again, or Tegernsee, or any of the beautiful countryside of Bavaria. If Mimmo and I had continued our romance, perhaps I would have gone to visit him there, but that's finito, and I can't imagine that I would have any reason to return. As difficult as many of the trips were, and as ill as Farrah often was, we had some good times. The walks along the lake, the wonderful dinners at Mimmo's, our snowball fight in the mountains, Farrah's birthday party, watching movies and drinking hot chocolate in her room, piled on the bed together.

Just waking up in the mornings and opening the curtains, seeing the beautiful snow-capped mountains and the sparkling lake, or the bright green of the grass in the springtime and the flowers blooming everywhere.

But most of all, I miss the closeness I shared with Farrah. We bonded in a way I've never experienced before. I've kept so much bottled up inside me for so long, but as I lay there trying to meditate, the tears finally came. I miss the way things were. At times, when I'm trying to remember something we did or how something transpired, I'll want to call Farrah and ask her because I know she would remember. But then I realize that she's not in a condition to have that conversation. She wouldn't be able to remember, and that makes me incredibly sad. I can't call my friend anymore when I need advice or an opinion or a laugh. The other day in the hospital, she looked at me and asked, "Where am I?" I know it's all the medication, and when they are able to decrease it, she's much more herself. But I understand what Ryan means when he says, "I want her back." So do I.

◈ *June 11, 2009*

I picked up Mexican food again and went to the hospital. I got there a little late because of bumper-to-bumper traffic, and Ryan had already left. Again I had enough food for an army and it was only Farrah, me, and Jennifer, the nurse. Farrah was having trouble breathing because of the fluid in her lungs. They're going to put her out and drain them tomorrow, but for tonight she's pretty much out of it on the pain medication. She couldn't really get her words out, and I didn't want her to struggle trying to talk to me. I could see by her eyes that she wanted to communicate, but she couldn't. I kissed her gently on the forehead and told her to sleep and I left. Honestly, I couldn't have stayed any longer. I've been refusing to give up on that possible miracle, but tonight the chances seemed very remote. I felt sad, discouraged, and even a little hopeless. Where is my dogged determination that she can get well?

I was speaking to a friend today and he said, "Sometimes you have to give them permission to go. Maybe they want to, but they're trying to hang on because they know their loved ones want them to. They have to know it's okay to let go." That took me by surprise. I'd never thought about it that way. I just assumed that we all had to keep cheerleading and encouraging her and telling her she's going to make it. Then I happened to speak to another friend, who told me a similar story about her father: He was in a coma and close to dying but still holding on. Someone told her she had to give him permission to go if that was what he wanted. When she did that, he rallied the next day and became very lucid and focused. He opened his eyes and smiled a warm, clear smile for the first time in two weeks. Twenty-four hours later he died, very peacefully.

Are we keeping her selfishly? Ryan said yesterday he would keep her like this forever, just to have her. I feel the same, but is it fair to her? What does she want? I don't think she's given up. She's a fighter and she's still so strong, it's as if none of these setbacks is enough to take her. I've never looked at this whole side of it.

Maybe she's just tired. I know I am. A deep-to-the-bone emotional and spiritual exhaustion. It's hard to see my friend lying there unable to move, struggling for breath, unable to eat, and seemingly wasting away. It's heartbreaking. I wonder what she thinks, what she wants . . .

### June 14, 2009

I went to the hospital this evening. Ryan and I had arranged to go at the same time; I think we probably need each other for strength right now. When I walked in he was leaning over and whispering tenderly to her. When he saw me, he said, "Darling, look who's here."

I stroked her head gently and said softly, "Hi, honey . . ." She stared at me with her large luminous eyes, but didn't speak . . . The look in her eyes was almost haunted. She was frail and gaunt, her tiny arms lying outside the covers but not moving. Often she takes my hand, but it was clear she didn't have the strength tonight. Ryan sat on the window seat next to Jennifer, the nurse, and they talked about the Lakers game. We had just won the championship. The television was still on, and we could see people celebrating. Jennifer said she and Farrah had watched the game and when the Lakers beat the Orlando Magic to take the title, Farrah managed to lift her fist in a gesture of victory. It's evident she understands what's going on but is so weak that she can barely speak. She rubbed her lips together in that gesture she always makes when they're dry. I asked, "Honey, do you want some of your lip cream?"

"No, thank you," she answered in a whisper, slowly forming the words. I didn't want to tax her by continuing to talk. I went into the bathroom and braced myself against the sink. I stared into the mirror, tears forming in my eyes. I needed to escape, to pull myself together. I didn't know what to say or how to act. After a few moments, I flushed the toilet and came back out. Ryan was leaning over her again, talking softly. I sat with Jennifer and asked mundane, meaningless questions. "Did she eat today?" "Did Dr. Piro say when she can come home?" I'd spoken to him this morning and he'd said hopefully midweek, so I already knew the answer, but I felt compelled to make some kind of small talk.

Farrah's eyes were starting to close, so Ryan kissed her tenderly and said, "Go to sleep now. I'll see you tomorrow." He made a heart gesture and mouthed, "I love you," to her. I could feel the tears starting to form again.

I kissed her forehead and whispered, "Goodnight, I'll see you tomorrow. I love you," but her eyes were already closed. Ryan and I walked out to the parking lot together. I gestured to the bench by the attendant's booth.

"Do you want to sit for a minute?" I asked. I needed to talk about Farrah, to stay there close to her for a while longer. We sat on the bench, discussing possible scenarios. I'm the one who's usually the cheerleader, but after seeing her tonight, I felt sort of resigned.

"She'll never leave here," Ryan whispered sadly.

"But maybe she'll rally?" I said. "She has before, you know . . ." I said it without much conviction this time. We sat there, sometimes talking, sometimes in silence. I told him the story about going shopping for her Mercedes after one of the bad-news scans, and how, when the man asked her if she wanted a two- or three-year lease, she'd made a kind of joke about it. We talked and even laughed some about our girl. "Our girl," he always calls her.

I came home and petted my dogs for a long time. They haven't gotten much attention from me lately. I didn't turn on the television, for a change, but put on some soft classical music, lit the candle in my bathroom, and got into a hot bath. I lay there for a long time, thinking about my friend . . . my beautiful friend. How could this have happened to her? I thought back over all the events of these past two years as I soaked in the soothing water. Where has the time gone? Two years ago today, she, Ryan, and I were at the clinic, her first trip there. It seems a lifetime ago. Lolita came in and lay down beside the tub, something she never does. She could feel my sadness. It felt like I had an ocean of tears inside me, but they were locked up too tightly to escape.

What will happen now? I don't feel optimistic about the coming days, but she's rallied before, my friend. As I said to Ryan tonight, "Farrah never likes to do the expected. She likes to be unpredictable. Maybe she'll surprise us . . ." I hope so. I'm going to sleep now, or at least I'll try to, but I'll leave my phone on as always.

*June 15, 2009*

I got a phone call from Ryan today to tell me Farrah was being moved to the ICU because her blood pressure was so low. He was completely choked up. It didn't sound good at all. I said I would get ready and come to the hospital right away but he said he'd call me from there once she'd been moved. I called Dr. Piro, who said to wait a couple of hours so they could get her settled in. The ICU has all these rules about visiting, so I had to wait until eight thirty to go. She was lying there looking small and frail, yet her face, as skeletal as it is now, still looked beautiful.

I sat by her bed and stroked her arm as she looked at me. An almost otherworldly stare. I needed to tell her some things before it was too late. "Honey," I said, "I never really tell you how much you mean to me, but I love you so much. Like a sister."

She looked up at me and said softly, "More than a sister . . ."

My eyes welled up with tears as I continued. "If I've ever said or done anything that hurt you in any way, I want you to know I'm so sorry. I'm so sorry we had that fight in the car on the way to the airport." I was openly crying now. I could tell by her eyes that she understood every word.

Then, I added, "And I want to thank you for being my friend and for all you've done for me. For letting me be a part of the documentary. It's touched so many people, Farrah. You can't imagine what a wonderful thing you've done . . ." She softly said, "Ohhh, honey," and with tremendous effort raised her frail little arms to hold me. We held each other for a long time, and afterward I looked at her and said, "You're tired, aren't you? This has been a long few years." She looked up at me and nodded. "Yes." I knew I had to ask her: "Do you still want to keep fighting?" She said softly, "Yes."

"Good," I said, "because if you do, we're fighting with you, but if you get too tired, that's okay, too." She looked at me and nodded. I kissed her forehead and we were silent for a while. I felt like I'd said what I needed to say. She knew we were behind her, whatever she chose to do.

Mela came into the room soon after with some fan letters she'd picked up at the apartment and two of Farrah's rosaries. "Can I join the party?" she asked. I think Farrah was happy to have her girls gathered around her. I talked about some of our Germany trips and the cocktail we always drank on Lufthansa. Farrah clearly said, "Why can't we have one?" We laughed about how Farrah always falls asleep the minute she gets into a car or anything that moves. We said, as soon as she was better, we'd take that Texas road trip and Mela would help me drive. I told Farrah that a very important magazine was doing a cover on her and she said, "They are?" I nodded, and continued, "And there's talk that you might win an Emmy for the documentary."

"Really?" She seemed surprised. Farrah was always surprised when she got accolades for her work. Then she said, barely coherent now, "I don't like them . . ."

"Who don't you like?" I asked.

Very faintly, she tried to get the words out: "That magazine."

"Oh, right," I said. "You were upset with them because you

thought they said something about you a long time ago?" Farrah raised her hand and made a "F— you" sign. Mela and I both laughed. That was Farrah, defiant to the end.

## June 20, 2009

I woke up this morning thinking about Farrah. There doesn't seem to be much time that I'm not thinking about her. I'll go up to see her today. I haven't been to the hospital for the past two days because I've been sick and didn't want to give her anything. Everyone here seems to be sick. Ryan is sicker than I've ever seen him. He's had a terrible flu the last few days. Farrah and I used to laugh about how strong he is. She'd say, "If Ryan gets a cold, it lasts about a minute." Even when he was diagnosed with leukemia, they came out with a drug a few weeks later that put it right into remission. He's still in remission after eight years. I sometimes forget he has cancer, too. I don't like to think about it. Ryan is indestructible. Isn't he? He has to be. I couldn't even face the thought of him getting sick.

Before I went to sleep last night I called Dr. Jacob in Germany. Maybe I'm grasping for one last straw, but I feel like I can't give up yet. I told her how Farrah is doing, and she said, "It doesn't sound good, Alana."

"Can't anything be done? I feel like she's just lying there dying. Isn't there something you can do?" She could hear the frustration and desperation in my voice.

"She should have this new antibody that they've just approved in Germany, but she can't have it while she's in the hospital. She would have to come home first."

"Can it help at this late stage?" I asked.

"They've just had a conference on it in Florida, and it has been quite successful in arresting very late stages of cancer. It's just been approved here in Germany but it still isn't approved in the States," she explained.

"This is crazy," I said, exasperated. "If there's something that might possibly help her, let's give it to her. She's just going to lie there and die and they'll just keep her drugged and comfortable until she goes. I'll give her the damn shots myself if I have to. How do we get it?"

"We will have to wait until she gets home. Nothing can be done while she's in the hospital, Alana." I could tell she was also frustrated.

Right. Of course. Better she should just have lots of pain medication and go peacefully. What if she doesn't want to go? Especially if there's something else left to try. A very slim chance, maybe, but still a chance. I almost wish we'd stayed in Germany. At least I feel they're more proactive there. And what if I did give her this new drug myself and what if she died? Would I be arrested for murder? How does that work? Okay, I realize I can't do something like this on my own, but it makes me crazy. There's something that might help her and we can't get it to her. Dr. Piro says she's in such a weakened state that giving her something new might push her over the edge. Her body seems to be failing, and something that causes a reaction, even though it would have a good result if she could tolerate it, might kill her. Would I want to take that chance? Would I want that responsibility on my shoulders? Mela and I talked about it last night. If there's a chance it could help pull her out of this, she feels we should do it, no matter what. She thinks it's worth it, and I think I do, too. What is there to lose? She can't and won't go on much longer like this. I wish she were able to make this decision herself. I know what she would do, though. I already know.

### June 22, 2009

This will be my last entry. The doctor said that it's only a matter of time, and I can't bring myself to write anymore. It seems this journey is almost over. I'm no longer numb. Crying is much easier lately; in fact, I'm surprised I have any tears left in me.

I went to the hospital tonight to see "our girl." As I pulled the chair close to her bed, Farrah opened her eyes and smiled slightly. "How are you, honey?" I asked as I held her hand and stroked it. She just stared into my eyes. I could see she wanted to say something, but she couldn't get the words out. I continued to hold her hand, and I stroked her soft, wispy hair with my other hand.

"Your hair is getting longer," I said. "It's this long now." I held up my finger and thumb about two inches apart. She tried to lift her hand to her head, but she couldn't quite make it.

"Do you want me to read the Lord's Prayer?" I asked. I showed her the Christian Science book that I often bring. "Yes," she answered softly. I read to her for a while, first the prayer, then Psalm 23 and several other passages. I put the book away and took her hand again. I could tell she was thinking about something. She tried to form a word with her lips but couldn't manage it. I said, "I wish I could read your mind." Her eyes looked momentarily frightened, and I wanted to ask, "Are you afraid?" but I wasn't sure if I should. I didn't know quite what to say; what was appropriate. Do you talk to a person about dying? Do you tell them not to be afraid, that it will be all right? Or do you just pretend everything is fine? I don't know ... I don't know. I wish someone would tell me.

She was still looking into my eyes as I was softly rubbing her arm. I had this urge to tell her about my upcoming biopsy at UCLA; that my Pap smear had come back irregular and that they are going to have to put me under and do a surgical procedure in order to get a proper biopsy. It's a year ago exactly that we were in Germany and I had the "cancer for a day." I wanted to tell her that I'm kind of nervous but that didn't seem appropriate, either, after what she's been through. I had this maudlin thought that maybe if it was positive, I'd be joining her in the not too far-off future. I sure couldn't do what she has done. Nor would I want to.

Finally, the nurse came in and gave her the pain medication, and soon her eyes were closing. I kissed her on the forehead. Then I remembered. "When they move you out of ICU, I asked if they could put a cot in your room so I can spend the night. We'll have a slumber party." She opened her eyes and tried to say something, but nothing came out. I kissed her again and said goodnight. I walked alone out into the balmy June night. I wondered how Ryan was doing. Redmond. Her daddy, Jimbo. How will they all make it through this? How will I?

**Farrah Fawcett passed away on June 25, 2009.**

# THE FINAL CHAPTER

W HERE DO I GO FROM HERE?
My thoughts have been filled with Farrah for such a long time that I'm not sure what I'll think about now. I guess it's not as easy as that. It seems she's all I think about. I go to sleep thinking about her and I wake up thinking about her. A huge, gaping hole has been left in my life and my heart. Who will I laugh with and complain to on the phone late at night? Who will I talk to about silly, superficial things—like hair, shopping, the latest bronzer? Who will I commiserate with when my kids are going through hard times? Or when I'm dating someone (if I ever do again!) and I want her wise and always insightful take on it? And saddest of all, who will I make pecan pies with when the holidays roll around? During the last couple of years, when our conversation was dominated mainly by cancer, Farrah and I always found something to laugh about. I believe that's one of the reasons Farrah was able to keep up her fight for so long; her humor, as well as her indomitable spirit and dogged determination, pulled her through and defied the odds. Until now.

When I embarked on this journey with her, neither of us

had any idea where the path would lead. We hoped we were steering toward a happy ending, a cure for her cancer. But in not knowing, we put our faith in medicine, God, and each other. This experience has changed my life forever, and the lessons that eluded me in the past are finally sinking in. I wish I could wrap them all up in neat little packages and give them to my children for Christmas, so that they don't have to learn them the hard way.

I have learned that you must live life fully and appreciate every precious minute. Your life can change in the blink of an eye; you never know what tomorrow holds, so you have to stay in the present. I've spent so much time regretting the past or fearing the future that I've rarely enjoyed just being here in the moment. I think of all the times when my kids have called and I've been in a rush and I didn't give them my full attention. Or when I've been too tired to cook a Sunday family dinner. Or when my dogs came to me, tails wagging, longing for my affection, and I gave them a quick pat as I dashed out the door. Moments I can never retrieve. I know now that you must cherish the people you love and spend all the time that you can with them—quality time.

A therapist once told me that he'd been with many people when they died and never once, in their last moments, did anyone talk about how many Ferraris they had owned or how many houses they had or how much money they had accumulated. He said it was always about how much they had loved or been loved. He said that love is all you remember; love is all that counts.

Being with Farrah these past several years has opened my heart and taught me the meaning of unconditional love in a way I haven't experienced since my children were born. And as I've watched my beautiful friend slip away, I've realized how important it is not only to open your heart and love deeply and fully but to tell the people you love how much they mean to you. I'm so glad I had the chance to do that with Farrah before the end. I only wish I had told her more often. Friendship with a woman is right up there with your relationship with your mate and your children. Maybe there was a time in my past when I wasn't always the best friend I could be, but from now on I will be. I realize the value and importance of it, and what a gift a true friend is.

Something else I've learned from my journey with Farrah is that we all have a source of inner strength to call upon, no matter what difficulties we may be facing. During this time with her, I've found myself in circumstances where I felt momentarily terrified— completely unequipped to face what was before me. I've had to dig down deep and find that inner strength that we all have. I believe that it comes from a Higher Power or God or whatever one chooses to call this force greater than we are. Now I know that this source gives me strength and courage to face whatever challenges may arise.

I've spent so much of my life in fear; mostly about my children or my future. Farrah was not a fearful person. She faced life head-on, and even though there were times she was obviously afraid, she did what she had to do with courage and dignity. David Kessler, a wonderful writer and motivational speaker, once said something in one of his talks that has stuck with me forever: "Fear doesn't stop you from dying; it stops you from living."

In going on this journey with Farrah I made a conscious decision: to put my friend's needs before my own; to put my problems on the back burner and to focus on what I had to do to help her. It's the oldest spiritual principle in the world. Kabbalah says that the only path to true joy and fulfillment is by becoming a being of sharing; it's more than just doing good deeds—it's a shift in consciousness. A shift from "What's in it for me?" to "How can I be of service?" From "What can I get?" to "What can I give?"

When I did this, something remarkable happened: my life transformed and many of my problems were solved; the Universe worked them out for me in ways I had never dreamed possible. I was talking to our friend Mela the other day and saying that I felt guilty that good things were happening in my life while we were losing Farrah. She said, "No, that's not it at all. This is what Farrah would have wanted for you. Maybe somehow she's had a hand in all this. It's her gift to you." I know she was right.

I started out wanting to "save" my friend. I wasn't successful—none of us was. And it will sadden me forever. Yet she's saved me in so many ways. And now, Ryan and I both will carry on her legacy as best we can. I'll continue to be her voice and fight for alternative treatments for cancer. I'll help in any way that I can to raise money for her foundation for cancer research. She's given so much to the world, and the least we can do is to keep her flame burning. I know it will anyway. The world will never forget Farrah Fawcett. I know I certainly won't.

> A friend loveth at all times.
> —PROVERBS 17:17

# ACKNOWLEDGMENTS

To Ryan O'Neal, my eternal gratitude to you for encouraging me, supporting me, and cheering me on during a most difficult and painful time for both of us. I feel that we are truly family now. I will always be on your team.

To Sheryl Berk, with my deepest gratitude for your tireless dedication, late nights, and your good-natured attitude—even in the most harried of deadlines. When I say I couldn't have done this book without you, I really mean it.

To the best literary agent in the world, Frank Weimann, my deepest appreciation to you for believing in me so wholeheartedly and being available any time of the night or day for my endless phone calls.

To Marianne Williamson, who has been my loving friend and spiritual mentor, and has always assured me and encouraged me that I could—and should—do this.

To the publishing team at HarperCollins: Lisa Sharkey, Matt Harper, Amy Kaplan, thank you for your faith in this book and me, and for convincing me that I could meet deadlines that were almost inhumanly possible.

To Dr. Ursula Jacob, Dr. Lawrence Piro, Dr. Thomas Vogl,

and Dr. Claus Kiehling: thank you for your dedication and compassion. And most of all, for how much you cared for Farrah.

To Paul Bloch and Arnold Robinson, thank you for your wonderful advice and support.

To Christine Romeo, for your assistance throughout this process.

To all my friends and family, whom I haven't always been available to for these last three years. Thank you for understanding. I love you all.

And last but not least, to George Hamilton, for having always encouraged me to write.